TORONTO

A SHORT ILLUSTRATED HISTORY OF ITS FIRST
12,000 YEARS

RONALD F. WILLIAMSON, EDITOR

JAMES LORIMER & COMPANY LTD., PUBLISHERS
TORONTO

James Lorimer & Company Ltd., Publishers acknowledge the support of the Ontario Arts Council. We
acknowledge the support of the Government of Canada through the Book Publishing Industry
Development Program (BPIDP) for our publishing activities. We acknowledge the support of the
Canada Council for the Arts for our publishing program. We acknowledge the support of the
Government of Ontario through the Ontario Media Development Corporation's Ontario Book Initiative.

 Canada Council   Conseil des Arts
for the Arts   du Canada

ONTARIO ARTS COUNCIL
CONSEIL DES ARTS DE L'ONTARIO

Visual co-ordinators: Andrea Carnevale and Kate Hoffmann

Library and Archives Canada Cataloguing in Publication

Toronto : a short illustrated history of its first 12,000 years / edited
by Ronald F. Williamson.

ISBN 978-1-55277-007-8

1. Toronto (Ont.)—History.   I. Williamson, R. F. (Ronald F.)
FC3097.4.T64 2008   971.3'541   C2007-907495-2

James Lorimer & Company Ltd., Publishers
317 Adelaide Street West, Suite 1002
Toronto, Ontario
M5V 1P9
www.lorimer.ca

Printed in China

TORONTO

CONTENTS

Acknowledgements

This volume began as an initiative of the City of Toronto through the offices of Heritage Toronto, and we thank the current and immediate past board and staff of Heritage Toronto for their support and encouragement. We are also grateful to Andrea Carnevale and Kate Hoffmann for their substantial efforts in the coordination of the visuals. While Mary MacDonald, Lillian Petroff, David Robertson and Andrew Stewart all made significant contributions to the direction and content of the book, we extend our special thanks to Randall White for his formative contributions of ideas and text in the early stages of the project. We are also grateful for the skilful editing of Lynn Schellenberg and Janet Shorten, whose efforts greatly improved the quality of the volume.

LIVING IN THE MIDDLE GROUND

Torontonians have long had a variety of interesting places to gather to enjoy their city, as these historical images witness. Left: Scarborough Beach Park's boardwalk, 1910. Middle: A peak along the Scarborough Bluffs. Right: Streetcars stopping at the CNE grounds.

The story of how Toronto became what it is today is contained in the pages of this book. As readers will discover, it is the ecological character and cultural diversity of this place that has defined its history. Not only is it situated on the shores of one of the largest freshwater lakes in Canada, but the Greater Toronto Area is defined by such natural features as the Niagara Escarpment, the Oak Ridges Moraine, assorted big and small lakes and a host of north-south rivers and creeks. Though from the air it may seem the city extends across flat land, anyone who has walked from the lakeshore up and across the old beachlines as far as Eglinton Avenue can understand why, in the winter, it can be raining on the waterfront and snowing in Lawrence Park. The differences in elevation are most apparent from the heights of the Scarborough Bluffs or the uplands above the Humber, the Don and the Rouge river valleys. These rivers, along with their associated estuaries, marshes, swamps, lakeshores, pondsides and steeply elevated uplands, have contributed to the shaping of Toronto and will continue to shape it in the future (even with the continuing rapid pace of real estate development).

This ecological diversity has been important to people for thousands of years. Many of our modern place names derive from the ancient languages of the original peoples and reflect significant environmental features of the area. The Mohawk word "Toronto" is one example.

People washing their cars in the Humber River in 1922.

Some people say that it means 'meeting place'; but others claim that 'it means trees standing in water,' and that the Mohawks used the word to refer to a productive fish weir at the Couchiching Narrows, where the water from Lake Simcoe flows north into the Severn River and on to Georgian Bay. (This would explain the labelling on some early French maps of present-day Lake Simcoe as *Lac Taronto* and of the eastern end of Georgian Bay as *Baye de Toronto*.)

Some three hundred years ago, the name Toronto was also applied to the Aboriginal canoe-and-portage route along the Humber and Holland Rivers known as *Le Passage de Toronto*, which served as a strategic transportation corridor between the upper and lower Great Lakes. Scholars still discuss and debate the exact historical use of this corridor during the "Indian-European" fur trade era, but the underlying geographic logic of the ancient Toronto Passage

is reflected in its successive modern reincarnations — from the earliest beginnings of Yonge Street in the late eighteenth century, to Toronto's first Northern Railway in the middle of the nineteenth century, and the present-day multi-lane Highway 400.

There are a number of ways in which both the historical and the present-day Toronto can be understood as a "middle ground." Its geography has served as a point of economic and cultural exchange among Canada's vast natural resource wilderness, such Atlantic Ocean seaports as New York and Montreal and the sprawling continental Midwest. Today, not only does one-third of the population of Canada live within a 160-kilometre radius of downtown Toronto, but one-third of the US population lies within a day's drive.

Our views of history are always changing; in response to contemporary developments, we see the past in new and more revealing lights. The enormous growth in the cultural plurality of Toronto that occurred in the last half of the twentieth century reminds us of the extent to which this place functioned as a middle ground among various peoples in the more distant past. Indeed, successive migrations of people from other places shaped life along the Toronto Passage for centuries before the arrival of European or "Euro-American" newcomers in the late nineteenth century. The city of today,

Downtown Toronto as viewed from the Island.

where at least 150 languages and dialects are spoken by people from all over the global village, is in some ways a quite new kind of place, mirroring stimulating developments in the evolution of the world at large. But there are various intriguing ways in which the Toronto region has long been a cultural middle ground — a place where different peoples have met and mingled, learning from each other and prospering, both economically and socially.

In the end, the interconnectedness of the diverse cultural and natural environments characterize the experiment that daily shapes the present-day city of Toronto and its surrounding region. In this spirit of living in the middle ground, five scholars with interests and expert knowledge of the city's past have sketched, with comparatively few words but many evocative illustrations, the story of how Toronto came to be what it is today. It is a tribute to the depth and development of the heritage community in the city and their work that we have been able to tell such a broad story of our city's past.

The much-admired former mayor David Crombie recently gave the William Kilbourn lecture on the future of Toronto, at the beautifully restored Elgin Winter Garden theatre on Yonge Street. It made for a memorable evening, full of the warm feelings that many Torontonians — old and new — harbour for the city in which they live. One of the things Crombie suggested was that, while the traditional annals of Toronto are undoubtedly interesting and remarkable, the city has reached a point where it needs to start re-imagining its history, using its past to meet the challenges of a new era in Canada, North America and beyond. It is our hope that this book will somehow be at once educational and entertaining, representing a modest contribution to our local re-imagining enterprise — yet another step in Toronto's ongoing adventure in city-building.

Peter J. Carruthers
Former Chair, Heritage Toronto
June 2008

The city of Toronto skyline, framed by greenery in a park across Lake Ontario, here seems dwarfed by the lake's expanse.

Chapter 1

TORONTO'S NATURAL HISTORY

Robert I. MacDonald

View from the CN Tower looking northeast. Note the green canopy in the background.

Gazing out over Toronto today from the observation deck of the CN Tower, one is immediately struck by the surrounding cultural landscape: the hulking Rogers Centre, Exhibition Place, Roy Thomson Hall, the office towers of Bay Street, standing like stylized chrome-and-glass chess pieces, Union Station and the verdigris-covered peak of the Royal York Hotel, Harbourfront, the concrete ribbon of the Gardiner Expressway and the grid of city streets extending northward to the horizon. Looking northward on a summer's day, however, beyond the immediate crowd of tall buildings, this perspective also reveals an amazing canopy of green — the crowns of the many trees that grace the yards and boulevards of the neighbourhoods embracing the downtown core.

Nature, it seems, cannot be so easily subdued by asphalt and concrete. If one turns to the south, the juxtaposition of the cultural and natural landscapes is thrown into even sharper relief by the overwhelming majesty of Lake Ontario, where the mightiest ships appear like toys on a pond. While we may rarely contemplate the influences of the natural landscape on our excursions through the city, the urban fabric is itself draped over a much deeper, more ancient foundation. This foundation, consisting of the geological landforms, watersheds, soils, climate, plants and animals that make up the natural landscape, has had its own profound influence on the 11,000-year human history of the Toronto area. Natural history sets the stage for the stories of all the different people who have lived on this particular piece of ground.

GEOLOGY AND GLACIAL HISTORY

The bones of the earth creak and groan every now and then, rattling the dishes in our cupboards and nudging the pictures on our walls askew, but the bedrock foundation generally lies out of sight and out of mind in Toronto. It consists primarily of grey shales interbedded with siltstone, limestone and dolomite. These sedimentary rocks formed as bottom sediments in a shallow, subtropical sea between about 488 and 443 million years ago, during the Ordovician geological period. At that time, the land mass that would become North America straddled the equator as an extensive, submerged marine shelf, fringed by mountains and covered by vast oceans. Not until the Late Jurassic period, during the age of dinosaurs about 150 million years ago, would the North American continent begin to assume its current appearance and location as this vast tectonic plate gradually rose above the seas and moved northward. Now, deformed by tectonic forces and ground down by glaciers, the beds of the Ordovician sedimentary rocks underlying Toronto dip slightly to the southwest and a vast swale has been scoured from the softer shales,

forming a buried valley that runs northward through Toronto to Georgian Bay.

While the existence of this great valley has been surmised by geologists for decades, the precise topography of this and other bedrock landforms in the Toronto area remains something of a mystery. This is because, aside from major geological features such as the Niagara Escarpment and localized outcrops in deeply eroded river valleys, the bedrock has been mantled by unconsolidated deposits laid down during the glacial cycles of the last two million years, a geological period known as the Quaternary. It is primarily this blanket of sediments that defines the current terrain and soils.

Exposures of Quaternary sediments at the Scarborough Bluffs and the Don Valley Brickworks reveal over 100,000 years of geological history, beginning well before the start of the last major period of continental glaciation around 75,000 years ago. Included in this record of layered sediments are the advances and retreats of the Laurentide Ice Sheet, the three-kilometre-thick continental glacier that once covered northeastern North America. As the ice gradually flowed southward over thousands of years, it first spilled into the bedrock basins now occupied by the Great Lakes and then expanded beyond these basins, reaching its maximum southerly extent in Ohio around 20,000 years ago.

On its subsequent retreat, the continental glacier took the form of massive ice lobes along its southern margin, each originating within one of the major bedrock basins. From then until the ice's final withdrawal around 12,500 years ago, these lobes advanced and retreated, leaving behind a complex record of glacial deposits. Meltwater lakes and rivers, dammed up and then released by the shifting ice, also contributed to the moulding of the landscape. One of the most impressive landforms created by these forces in the Toronto area is the Oak Ridges Moraine,

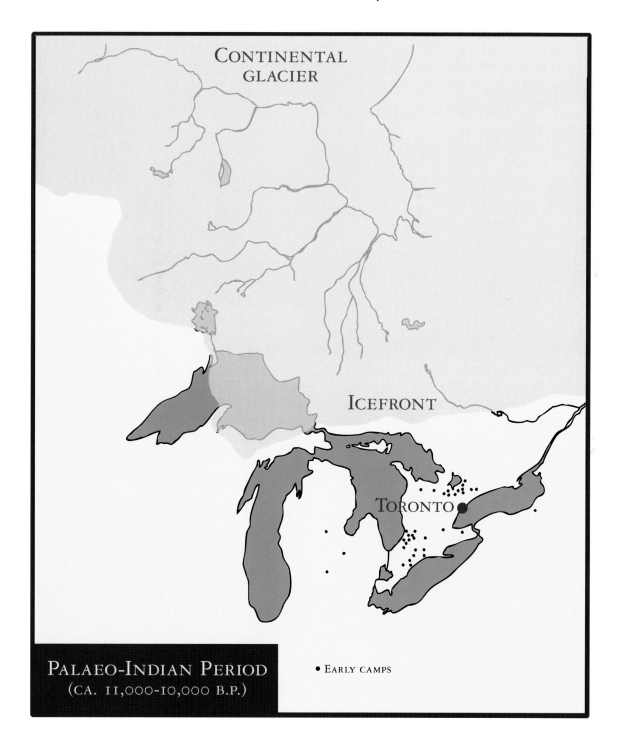

CONTINENTAL
GLACIER

ICEFRONT

TORONTO●

PALAEO-INDIAN PERIOD
(CA. 11,000-10,000 B.P.)

● EARLY CAMPS

Exposed layers of Quarternary sediments at the Don Valley Brickworks, shown here, reveal over 100,000 years of geological history. Students from Toronto-area schools visit the site on field trips to learn more about the formation of the area's current terrain and soils.

which extends across the north edge of the city from the Niagara Escarpment at Caledon East to near Castleton east of Rice Lake. Marking the position where two glacial lobes came together, one from the Lake Ontario basin and the other from the Lake Huron/Georgian Bay basin, this complex ridge was built from sediments laid down in rivers flowing under the ice, in fans and deltas that formed under water dammed between the ice and the Niagara Escarpment, and in flows of material from the margins of the ice. Today this feature forms the drainage divide between the Lake Ontario and Lake Simcoe/Lake Huron basins. Owing to the porosity of its sediments,

which allows precipitation to percolate into the ground, the Oak Ridges Moraine is also recognized as a significant groundwater source, feeding into tributaries throughout the present-day Greater Toronto Area.

Underlying and south of the Oak Ridges Moraine, the continental glacier laid down several deposits of glacial till, a poorly sorted sediment often containing boulders and gravel in a matrix of sand, silt or clay. These deposits were subsequently capped by a patchy veneer of silt and clay laid down in short-lived meltwater lakes. Together, these deposits mantle the bedrock at depths ranging from fifteen to more than two hundred metres. This is the South Slope Till Plain, a gently rolling landscape, inclined gradually towards Lake Ontario, where entrenched rivers and streams are the main sources of topographical relief. Driving north on Highway 400, one ascends this gently sloping plain before encountering the Oak Ridges Moraine north of King Road.

As the Ontario ice lobe retreated, the basin filled with water, creating glacial Lake Iroquois, around 12,500 years ago. Unable to find its current outlet, which remained blocked by glacial ice, Lake Iroquois drained via the Mohawk Valley through an outlet near what is now Rome, New York. The elevation of this outlet created a lake that was considerably higher than the current level of Lake Ontario. By the time the St. Lawrence River outlet opened up and Lake Iroquois began to drain, around 12,000 years ago, it had built an imposing shore bluff around the perimeter of its basin. In Toronto, this bluff, which averages about fifteen metres in height, is the familiar ridge upon which Casa Loma surveys the downtown. Davenport Road runs along the former beach below the bluff.

From the Lake Iroquois bluff to the Lake Ontario shore is the Iroquois Plain, a gently sloping plateau where earlier glacial deposits were exposed by wave action. Materials eroded from the Lake Iroquois bluff, as well as sedi-

One of Toronto's most spectacular natural features, the Scarborough Bluffs were formed around 13,000 years ago after the last ice age. The escarpment today stretches 14 kilometres along the shoreline of Lake Ontario.

ments transported into the lake by rivers and streams, were laid down as a relatively thin veneer over these earlier deposits. Coarser, heavier sands were laid down close to the Iroquois beach, while the finer, lighter silt and clay particles were carried farther out into the lake. From Erin Mills Parkway in the west to Warden Avenue in the east, shallow-water deposits of sand are the predominant Lake Iroquois sediments. East of the Rouge River, in Ajax, deep-water deposits of silt and clay are extensive.

The former shore of Lake Iroquois also features two large bays, one now occupied by Black Creek and the Humber River, and the other now occupied by the east and west branches of the Don River. Lakeshore currents moving in a westerly direction created large bars of sand and gravel across the mouths of these bays. The western bar is traversed by St. Clair Avenue from the

Geography professor W.A. Mahaney from York University navigates the bed of the Rouge River, one of Toronto's major watersheds. Geomorphologists such as Mahaney study landforms and the processes that shape them.

Humber River easterly to the Canadian National Railway tracks. The Lambton Golf and Country Club enjoys a view of the Humber River valley from its northern flanks. The eastern bar extends from near Coxwell Avenue, south of Danforth Avenue, east to Kennedy Road.

When Lake Iroquois drained, the water level in the Ontario basin initially fell to sea level. The weight of the continental glacier, several kilometres thick, had not only scoured the bedrock, but also depressed it. As the bedrock began to rise again — a process called isostatic rebound, which slowly continues to the present day — the outlet rose faster than the rest of the basin. This tilting of the basin gradually raised water levels again within early Lake Ontario. The process was slow, however, as landform changes elsewhere in the Great Lakes watershed caused flow from the upper Great Lakes to bypass lakes Erie and Ontario and go directly to the St. Lawrence River via the Ottawa Valley. It was not until around

5,000 years ago that full flow through the lower Great Lakes resumed, and water in Lake Ontario reached its current levels.

Several millennia before current lake levels were achieved, Lake Ontario began eroding the Quaternary deposits that comprise the Scarborough Bluffs. Lakeshore currents transported vast amounts of sediment to the west, where they were deposited in the lea of the point of land on which the R.C. Harris Filtration Plant stands today. Together with the outflow from the Don River, these deposits formed an enormous recurve sand spit. Substantial land filling and remodelling during the nineteenth and twentieth centuries roughly tripled its area. Known today as the Toronto Islands, it is the geological feature that created Toronto's natural harbour.

WATERSHEDS

The major watersheds of the present-day city of Toronto are, from west to east, Etobicoke Creek, Mimico Creek, the Humber River, the Don River, Highland Creek and the Rouge River. They all share a basic form, with their headwaters typically arising along the southern margin of the Oak Ridges Moraine. It is there that their slopes are steepest. They traverse the South Slope Till Plain in a roughly south-southeasterly direction along a moderate slope. They continue this course over the Lake Iroquois bluff, but having

A tranquil fall scene along the Humber River, not far from Lake Ontario in Etobicoke. Since earliest days a popular site for fishing, canoeing and other recreation, the Humber is another of the six major watersheds of present-day Toronto.

dropped to the Iroquois Plain their slopes become rather flat. Their overall form is branching, with many small tributaries fanning out across the headwaters, converging into a few major streams in the central sections, and finally merging into a single main branch with minor feeder streams in the lower sections.

During the millennia when the Toronto shore of Lake Ontario was lower and several kilometres south of its current location, the rivers cut down through the various Quaternary sediments as they flowed towards the lake, entrenching themselves in relatively deep valleys. Rising lake levels subsequently reduced the slope of these watercourses, creating extensive coastal wetlands at their drowned mouths and forcing them to meander and broaden their val-

leys. We see the result today in, for example, the Don River valley; while only 10 metres deep and 200 metres wide where the east branch crosses Highway 401, the valley grows to 30 metres deep and up to 750 metres wide as it approaches the mouth at Lake Ontario.

The character of these rivers and their tributaries has been severely obscured by land development, particularly within the urbanized lower sections. To get a sense of these landscapes as they once were, we must turn to historical accounts. The Don River, the central watershed of Toronto, illustrates what these accounts reveal.

In 1788, surveyor Alexander Aitkin noted that the Don was navigable upstream by boat for two or three miles from Lake Ontario. The upstream limit of commercial navigation at that time was

The Oak Ridges Moraine is characterized by hummocky terrain and vegetation adapted to dry conditions.

tured in the following description by W.H. Pearson in his book *Recollections and Records of Toronto of Old (1914)*:

The river was so very serpentine that one would have to go about three miles to one in a straight line. There were long stretches of meadow land between the windings of the river, and a good deal of marsh. This, as well as the marsh between the harbor and Ashbridge's Bay, was a great place for muskrats, and numbers were trapped.

near Danforth Avenue, where there was a ford that was part of a trail leading to Montreal. Conservationist and local historian Charles Sauriol, in his 1981 book *Remembering the Don*, notes that during the nineteenth century there was considerable traffic of schooners and smaller vessels to factory wharves in the vicinity of Gerrard Street. He also reports that pioneer records refer to the forks of the Don as the "boatbuildery," alluding to some degree of navigability farther upstream. Indeed, in the late eighteenth century, the North West Company used the lower Don as part of its fur trade route to Lake Simcoe and Georgian Bay. Small, shallow-draft boats were rowed upstream to the forks and then up the west branch to where the newly created Yonge Street intercepted the river at Hogg's Hollow (York Mills). From there the boats were lashed onto wheels and pulled overland to the Holland River.

The original character of the lower Don is cap-

In his 1873 history of Toronto entitled *Toronto of Old*, noted cleric and scholar Henry Scadding indicated that, as one progressed upstream, the marshes gave way to meadow at about the present location of Riverdale Park, approximately two kilometres inland. He too made note of the "morasses" that characterized Ashbridge's Bay and the contiguous marshes through which the Don flowed into Lake Ontario. The riverside marsh he describes as "one thicket of wild willow, alder, and other aquatic shrubbery," including witch hazel, dogwood, highbush cranberry, wild grape, blue iris, reeds and cattails. He refers as well to an island near the mouth of Castle Frank Brook where wild rice grew plentifully. W.H. Pearson also mentions "many stately elms" on the river flats, as well as wild plum, butternut, gooseberry and currants in abundance.

At their confluence, the course of the east and west branches of the Don is directed to the west

View of Toronto (1855) *by Mary Hastings Meyer. The artist painted this landscape from along the Don River, south of what is now Bloor Street.*

by the previously mentioned sand and gravel bar, which was formed at the mouth of the bay in glacial Lake Iroquois. In addition to this extensive bar deposit, most of the Iroquois Plain that flanks the lower Don Valley was capped by near-shore deposits of sand. This porous soil seems to have had considerable influence on the upland forest that surrounded the lower Don Valley. In the late eighteenth century, travelling to their summer retreat of "Castle Frank" near present-day Bloor Street and Bayview Avenue, Lieutenant-Governor and Mrs. Simcoe followed a trail along Yonge Street and then easterly to the Don, through shady pine plains covered with ferns. The summer home itself was situated on the edge of a plateau overlooking the Don Valley that was covered with white pines of huge girth. Mrs. Simcoe also reported visiting a farm at the current location of the Don Valley Brickworks,

which she described as being under a hill covered with pine. Reverend Scadding noted as well the predominance of mature pine in the uplands surrounding Castle Frank Brook, Todmorden Mills and the forks of the Don, and he completed the picture with the following description:

> Northward [from the Queen Street bridge], while many fine elms would be seen towering up from the land on a level with the river, the bold hills above them and beyond were covered with lofty pines. Southward, in the distance, was a great stretch of marsh, with the blue lake along the horizon. In the summer this marsh was one vast jungle of tall flags and reeds.

FLORA AND FAUNA

The historical distribution of vegetation in

Oak savannah is characterized by grassed land with widely spaced oak trees.

Toronto and its environs was the outcome of many centuries of adaptation, influenced by latitude, climate, topography and soils. It took several millennia for the major latitudinal forest zones of Ontario — the boreal forest in the north, the northern hardwood forest in the middle latitudes and the Carolinian forest in the south — to develop. During the last ice age these forest communities moved south in advance of the continental glacier, squeezing into much narrower latitudinal forest zones. As the climate warmed and the ice retreated, these communities expanded northward again. For a short time, the area we now call Toronto was carpeted by tundra vegetation that colonized the barren path of the retreating glacier. Later this vegetation was overtaken by a boreal forest dominated first by spruce

and later by pine. Gradually the deciduous species began to arrive, and by about 7,500 years ago the essentially modern forests had become established. Natural disruptions wrought by fire, wind, disease, pests and climatic change continued to create minor variations in the city's forest communities thereafter.

Toronto's climate is moderated by the proximity of Lake Ontario, and the northern edge of the Carolinian ecological zone skirts the shore of the lake. The Carolinian region is characterized by species of plants and animals with southern affinities; besides the beech and sugar-maple forests, which are the dominant forest communities in the zone, there are hickory and walnut trees, more frequently found to the south. Once, communities of oak, in association with hickory

Fishing by torchlight along the major rivers of the city was a common practice for thousands of years and into the colonial period.

and pine, were common on the porous sands of the Iroquois Plain. Nineteenth-century botanists described finding oak savanna, pine barrens and tallgrass prairie on very dry sites in the Toronto area. Remnants of these communities can still be found in Toronto, such as the oak savanna of High Park. North of Richmond Hill, where the climatic influence of Lake Ontario is reduced and the soils of the South Slope Till Plain are heavier, the pre-settlement canopy of maple and beech forest became more uniform. These northern hardwood-forest communities also frequently included basswood, elm, hemlock and white pine. Breaks in this canopy were limited to river valleys and areas where windstorms had blown down patches of forest. In contrast, the aptly named Oak Ridges Moraine was an area where porous soils favoured the growth of oak, although other communities that had adapted to the drier soils also existed there, including pine forest, oak savanna and prairie.

The diversity of vegetation communities in Toronto and the richness of the downstream riverside and coastal wetlands produced a broad range of habitats attractive to animals. Unlike the closed-canopy northern hardwood forest, where galleries of mature trees produced an impover-ished forest-floor plant community starved for

A southerly view of the Niagara Escarpment, with Lake Ontario on the horizon. The Niagara Escarpment is one of the natural features that define the Greater Toronto Area and exemplify its ecological diversity.

light, the Iroquois Plain offered wetland, upland forest, savanna and prairie habitats rich in food resources and protective cover. Herbivores, including mammals such as moose, elk, deer, beaver, muskrat and porcupine, and upland game birds, such as wild turkey and ruffed grouse, had an abundance of shrubs, saplings, grasses, nuts, seeds and wetland vegetation to feed on. These and other creatures in turn provided prey for carnivores and omnivores, such as bears, wolves, cougars, lynxes, martens, fishers, minks, river otters, raccoons and skunks. Waterfowl, reptiles and amphibians were more plentiful in the downstream riverside and coastal wetlands than in the smaller and seasonal watercourses of the interior.

Historical descriptions indicate that the Toronto area was characterized by three princi-pal fish habitats: alternating pools and riffles in the upper and middle river sections, the downstream riverside and coastal wetlands, and the deepwater habitat of Lake Ontario. Fish would have been most plentiful in the coastal marshes, which are among the most productive of all known ecosystems, thanks to the diversity of their habitat structure and the rejuvenating effects of natural fluctuations in lake water levels.

Two sorts of historical fisheries once existed within Toronto watersheds. The first group, comprising American eel, Atlantic salmon, lake whitefish and lake trout, were typically harvested during spawning runs in the fall. In the nineteenth century, Reverend Scadding reported that hundreds of salmon were taken annually from the Don River. A favourite fishing technique was jack lighting, using torches made from resinous pine knots mounted on the front of fishing skiffs to attract the salmon. On one such fishing expedition, Scadding and friends speared twenty large salmon in an hour. Historian Charles Sauriol reports that a settler in 1793 harvested ninety salmon near Castle Frank. The distance to which the salmon ran upstream can be gauged by a newspaper advertisement of 1798, listing for auction a farm on Yonge Street about twelve miles (or twenty kilometres) from York, which boasted an excellent salmon fishery large enough to support a number of families.

The second group of fish comprises brown bullhead, northern pike, sunfish, yellow perch and suckers. Resident populations of brown bullhead, suckers and yellow perch may have been available in the middle river sections year-round, while other populations of suckers and yellow perch, which were resident in the lower Don River or shallow waters of Lake Ontario, may have moved upstream during their annual spring spawning runs. Suckers are one of the few species tolerant enough of declining water quality to have managed to maintain resident populations in the Don River to the present, and Charles Sauriol notes that, within recent memory, the banks of the Don River by Pottery Road have been white with suckers stranded by falling spring water levels. Brown bullhead would have been much more abundant in the marshes of the lower Don and the Lake Ontario coast and were once caught by the tubful in the lower Don between Queen Street and Riverdale Park. Northern pike and sunfish tend to prefer the warmer waters, slower currents, and weedy habitat that characterized the coastal wetlands. According to W.H. Pearson, during the nineteenth century: "Pike, bass, perch, sunfish, and occasionally a maskinonge, were caught off the wharves and were quite plentiful in Ashbridges' Bay and the River Don." Larger pike, which generally prefer the deeper waters of the lake, may have been harvested

As shown in this photograph, salmon still run the Humber today, as at this weir at the Old Mill.

in the early spring when they migrated into the estuary and marshes to spawn. Today, Environment Canada rates the Don the lowest in Ontario for water quality, with only seven species of fish in the Toronto stretch of the river.

NATURE AND CULTURE

The bountiful Toronto fishery described in the written historical sources only chronicles the more recent exploitation of an ancient resource. For thousands of years before the arrival of European explorers and colonists, Aboriginal peoples were attracted to the north shore of Lake Ontario by its prodigious fishery and numerous other attractions. Many of their settlements now lie submerged on more ancient, lower-level beaches of Lake Ontario, while traces of others have been unwittingly eradicated by urban development. Nevertheless, some archaeological evidence survives to confirm the relationship between fishing as a major food-harvesting activity and early Aboriginal settlement locations.

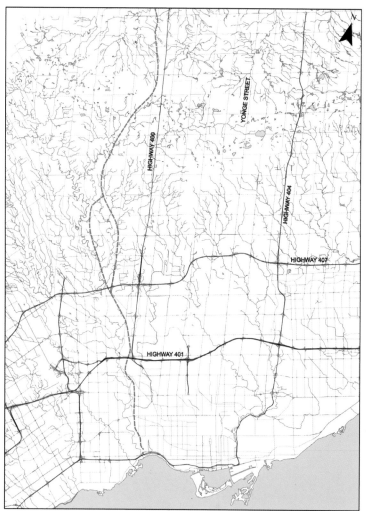

The Millennium Bridge on the Humber River. The Toronto Carrying Place Trail (marked in red, left) followed its river valley.

Archaeological evidence also shows how bands of hunter-gatherers used the Lake Ontario shore as part of a major canoe route that extended laterally along the major river systems. These routes, by canoe upstream as far as possible and then by foot trail along the river, connected Lake Ontario to Georgian Bay and Lake Huron via the Lake Simcoe watershed. Foremost among these was the Toronto Carrying Place Trail, or Toronto Passage, whose

main route followed the Humber River Valley northward over the drainage divide to the headwaters of the west branch of the Holland River. This trail, and its branches along the Don and Rouge rivers, not only served to connect these people with Aboriginal populations throughout the Great Lakes watershed, but also allowed them access to interior hunting grounds. Beginning around 1,600 years ago, when these people started growing crops to supplement hunting and gathering and began expanding their communities into the interior uplands, these same trails allowed them to maintain their connection to the ever-important coastal fishery and resources of the Iroquois Plain. Many of these Aboriginal trails, including Davenport Road below the Iroquois bluff, have evolved into modern roads, with their heritage barely remembered. All, however, are testaments to the structure and character of Toronto's natural landscape, and the way successive human populations have responded to it for more than 11,000 years. In many ways Toronto is a palimpsest, which has been overwritten time and time again by fresh waves of newcomers attracted to its rich and varied landscape.

Chapter 2

BEFORE THE VISITORS

Ronald F. Williamson

Before recorded history, the area now known as Toronto was a junction point of land and water routes, with trails along the rivers extending northward from the shoreline to link the lower and upper Great Lakes. For over ten millennia, encampments and temporary villages of various sizes were situated along the river valleys and the lakeshore. Few people are aware of the depth of this settlement history, or know about the societies that inhabited Ontario before the arrival of settlers from Europe and the United States about two hundred years ago. The Aboriginal occupants of these sites left no written record of their lives. Their legacy consists of the oral histories and traditions passed on to their descendants and the traces of their settlements that still survive today.

These traces form the local archaeological record, and they are far different from those portrayed in popular movies and television shows. Rather than ancient city temples filled with hidden treasure, these remains are often found in

This contemporary painting by Shelley Huson, modelled on the Red Hill Valley in Hamilton, illustrates how early hunters in the Toronto region would have sought high vantage points such as shoreline cliffs to track herds of caribou and other large game.

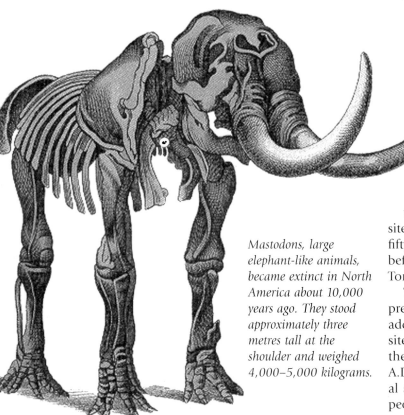

Mastodons, large elephant-like animals, became extinct in North America about 10,000 years ago. They stood approximately three metres tall at the shoulder and weighed 4,000–5,000 kilograms.

Deposits under the plough-zone soils remained largely intact. Extraordinary population growth after the First World War resulted in a more destructive trend, as urban growth consumed large tracts of cultivated land. The amount of site destruction brought about by that growth was astounding. In fact, while some sites are undoubtedly awaiting discovery, hundreds of sites have been destroyed in Toronto in the last fifty years and the record of what happened before Europeans arrived in the area that is now Toronto is incomplete and poorly understood.

The increasing role of Aboriginal people in preserving their past has helped governments address these trends. Most of the archaeological sites in Ontario were left by people living during the pre-European contact era (before about A.D.1600) and have distinct cultural and spiritual significance for their descendants. Aboriginal people today have a special interest in seeing that pre-contact archaeological sites are not sacrificed in the name of progress, and archaeologists are working more closely with First Nations today than ever before.

the trash deposits of the early inhabitants' dwellings. The challenge of the archaeologist is to bring this past to life by examining the artifacts that survive in today's altered landscape.

Archaeological sites are fragile and non-renewable. Today, provincial and municipal governments in Ontario consider it essential to conserve such sites, but that was not always the case. There were staggering losses to the archaeological record of Ontario during the past two centuries. The first period of disturbance to sites occurred when nineteenth-century European immigrants deforested and cultivated land for the first time. That disturbance, however, caused only partial destruction of archaeological information.

THE EARLIEST HUNTERS
(9000 B.C. – 7000 B.C.)

Aboriginal people are clear that they first inhabited this land, and Western science agrees. The archaeological record indicates that small bands of nomadic hunters moved into the Great Lakes region some 11,000 years ago, soon after the continental glacier retreated. During the previous millennia, southern Ontario was covered by glaciers that stretched across most of Canada and the northern continental United States. As these glaciers began to retreat approximately 14,000 years ago, large meltwater lakes formed in their

Caribou were among the main prey of the earliest hunters. Right: Hunters used stone points, such as these 11,000-year-old artifacts, to tip their spears. These points have flutes — large flakes struck from their bases — a feature only used for about eight hundred years.

wake and continued to cover much of southern Ontario. The people who came to live on the shores of these lakes pursued caribou, mastodon or mammoth (now-extinct elephants), and other game in what was then an open spruce forest mixed with tundra, similar to the environment found today in the subarctic region of Canada. Mammoth remains have been found in Toronto in several locations: substantial parts of skeletons were found during the excavation for the Eaton's store at College and Yonge streets and during sewer construction in 1910 near the intersection of Bathurst and Dupont streets. Other mammoth or mastodon remains have been found in sand and gravel deposits in the Christie Pits and in the former McCaul's sandpit on Weston Road near Bushy Avenue. Caribou remains, a flint spear point and a pestle were found in 1884 in a gravel ridge at a depth of twenty feet at the former Gunn's stockyard in West Toronto. While no definite evidence of human habitation was found along with these remains, archaeologists have discovered, at the Hiscock site, about one hundred kilometres east of Buffalo, 11,000-year-old spear points in association with some butchered mastodon bone that appears to have been fashioned into tools by humans. Most archaeologists believe that early hunters were indeed pursuing elephants in the Toronto area 11,000 years ago.

Evidence concerning these early hunters is very limited, since their populations were not large and since little of their material culture has survived the millennia. Also, in hunting herds of migratory caribou, their main prey, groups travelled long distances, even hundreds of kilometres over the course of a year, and seldom stayed in any one place for long. Their camps are frequently found near the now-abandoned and often elevated shorelines of large lakes, probably because they afforded views from which people could spot and intercept migrating caribou herds. The Lake Iroquois shoreline from about 12,500 years ago, which forms the bluff above Davenport Road, is one such relict shore, although it was located well inland by the time Toronto was first occupied. Dozens of 10,000- to 11,000-year-old artifacts have been found along this ancient shoreline in the municipalities that border the present city of Toronto. Residential backyards along this ridge are now among the best places to find evidence of the earliest occupants of Toronto, since the balance of this landform has been heavily disturbed by twentieth-century development.

The water levels in the Lake Ontario basin continued to fall just after the glaciers retreated before rising again to modern levels. Unfortunately, some of the largest campsites were along its shoreline and next to estuaries that drained into this early Lake Ontario. Many of these sites are now situated more than a kilometre into the lake.

Truly spectacular evidence of those submerged occupations surfaced in 1908 during tunnelling in Toronto Bay to the east of Hanlan's Point, at a depth of seventy feet below water level. This evidence consisted of over one hundred human foot (possibly moccasined) prints, and was one of the most important discoveries of that period made in America. The footprints had been found in a layer of blue clay about six feet wide by workers constructing a waterworks tunnel. Remarkably, these prints appeared to represent the steps of a family. W.H. Cross, the city inspector who witnessed the find, described it as follows:

> It looked like a trail . . . . You could follow one man the whole way. Some footprints were on top of the others, partly obliterating them. There were footsteps of all sizes, and a single print of a child's foot. . . . All of the footprints toed in and you could see the hollow between the ball and the heel in many of them . . . in some places you could see where the toe had been driven in and the clay had shot up under the heel.

A foreman with the construction company, William Axford, confirmed the statements of Cross, describing the footsteps as "clear as those made by a man's moccasined foot stamped into the stiff mud." Professor A.P. Coleman, a well-known geologist of the day, was consulted. While at the time Professor Coleman believed that the blue clay stratum dated to the interglacial period before the last glaciation, it is now thought that the clay was laid down during the Wisconsin glaciation, suggesting that the find may represent a family heading for downtown Toronto from their camp between 10,500 and 11,000 years ago.

Although few of the earliest hunters' camps have ever been found, the locations where many of their spear points were lost or broken (and sometimes repaired) during hunting have been documented. Archaeologists can readily identify their stone tools and the by-products of their flaked stone industry. Their distinctive spear points were made from chert or flint. Flint is chemically similar to glass, being composed largely of the mineral silica, and so it can be worked into complex shapes by flaking or chipping it along the edges. An experienced flintknapper, by removing flakes from the edge of a piece of flint, can produce any number of shapes. The stone tools that date to this and subsequent periods include such implements as knives, projectile points (spear, javelin and arrow heads), drill bits, various scrapers and engraving tools.

Sometimes, by analyzing the wear patterns and organic residues on tools themselves, archaeologists can determine how they were used. One fluted tool at the Hiscock site, for example, was found to have traces of musk-ox or bison blood along its edges. Archaeologists can also identify when and where artifacts were made by examining their size, shape and "style." The distinctive spear points of this period, for example, are characterized by a prominent channel or groove on each face, called a flute. This is a stylistic (perhaps also functional) attribute that appears on spear points across North America, but only between 10,500 and 11,000 years ago.

THE CHANGING ENVIRONMENT — HUNTERS, GATHERERS AND FISHERS (7000 B.C.–1000 B.C.)

By 9,000 years ago, southern Ontario had changed from a tundra-like environment to one covered by mixed needle and broadleaf forest. The nomadic hunter-gatherers had to adapt to the changing environmental conditions. They harvested new plants and hunted animals, while still moving long distances over the land during the course of a year. The landscape in which these people lived continued to change: water levels lowered in the Great Lakes and temperate forests expanded. As a result of the changes in their environment over the following millennia, their

hunting strategies shifted, and their toolkits became more varied. By four to five thousand years ago, small bands of related families had settled into familiar hunting territories. Their annual seasonal round of travel involved occupation of two major types of sites. In large spring and summer settlements, located near river mouths, many groups of families came together to take advantage of aquatic resources such as spawning fish. They also came to these sites to trade, and to bury their dead, sometimes with elaborate mortuary ceremonies and offerings. In the fall and winter, small groups of related families occupied small camps in the forested interior to harvest nuts and to hunt deer that browsed in the forests or congregated in cedar swamps during the winter.

The lakeshore and estuary sites associated with

This 700-year-old ceramic effigy pipe, found at an archaeological site just west of the current city boundary, seems to have been in the form of a pregnant woman. The figure has a basket strapped to its back that functioned as the bowl of the pipe.

An ancestral Huron site near Toronto. Archaeological sites are often found by spotting artifacts on the surface of freshly ploughed fields. The extent of the artifact scatter closely approximates the size of the site.

this seasonal round are now either submerged or buried under modern landfill. Some of the interior sites survive, however, especially along the middle reaches of the Humber River, where archaeologists have found 3,000- to 5,000-year-old artifacts in an area known as the Eglinton Flats. The artifacts are spear points made from Onondaga chert, a stone that was quarried along the north shore of Lake Erie. Some of the pieces appear to have been damaged by extreme heat, perhaps because they were discarded in a campfire. Unfortunately, few details of the sites at which these points were found have survived.

There are better records, however, for a recently documented site at James Gardens on the west bank of the Humber River, just south of Eglinton Avenue between Royal York Road and Scarlett Road. During the 1920s, while installing weeping tiles and several water features (still present in the gardens today), Frederick James uncovered twelve stone tools, also made of Onondaga chert, most of which have the same size and form and indi-

cate there is an important, still largely undisturbed 4,000-year-old site on the property.

An even older site existed on Deerlick Creek, a tributary of the Don River. Mima Kapches of the Royal Ontario Museum investigated the site and found that it had been occupied several times, including on one occasion 6,700 years ago when a small stone pebble with a human effigy was left behind. An isolated 2,500-year-old, exquisitely flaked preform for a spear point was also recovered from the campsite, indicating repeated uses of this place over thousands of years.

Other ancient artifacts have been found in the former Scarborough Township (now in the east end of Toronto). At several farms near the Scarborough Bluffs, landowners have found a 9,500 to 10,000-year-old spear point, a 7,000-year-old spear point, and several 4,000-year-old stone tools, including groundstone axes. A 7,000-year-old spear point was also found by archaeologists during excavations at the site of York's first general hospital at the intersection of

King and John streets, now home to the Toronto International Film Festival.

Most of these sites have not been professionally explored, but in other municipalities nearby, archaeologists have conducted detailed excavations at a number of sites that range in age from nine to three thousand years old. Many visitors to archaeological site excavations in the Great Lakes region are surprised to find that archaeologists dig to within only twenty to thirty centimetres of the surface. They are no doubt accustomed to seeing or imagining much deeper excavations in places like the Middle East or Mesoamerica, as depicted in the popular media. What they soon learn is that, in most cases, the ground surface we are walking on today is essentially the same surface that these early hunter-gatherers were walking on thousands of years ago. Only in places like river floodplains, where additional sediment has built up over time, do archaeological sites exhibit deep layering.

The first step in the excavation of any archaeological site is to establish a series of fixed reference points, which form a grid pattern. The grid allows archaeologists to accurately position their excavation squares and to record and map their finds. Recording such details during the collection of artifacts from archaeological sites is critical. Without secure knowledge of the context of finds, their significance is seriously compromised and they are little more than historical curiosities.

All of the soil from excavated squares is screened through six-millimetre mesh to recover artifacts, such as flaked and ground stone tools, carved and drilled bone artifacts, and food refuse in the form of butchered animal bones. Also, as the topsoil is removed from a site and the buff-coloured subsoil exposed, black stains of various sizes are revealed. The largest of these stains are pit features, holes that the inhabitants of the site dug to store food or discard refuse or to serve

James Gardens. In the 1920s, James uncovered twelve stone tools on his land, including this spear point, right. The property, now a public park, contains an important 4,000-year-old and largely undisturbed site.

some other function. Some of the pits contain red soil, where the heat of cooking fires burned and discoloured the natural soil, while others are grey, containing large quantities of ash. In the case of many of these pit features, archaeologists collect samples of soil and then subject them to a process called flotation, which isolates carbonized plant remains. They then examine these remains microscopically to identify specific plant species and to determine which plants were part of the site inhabitants' diet. The animal bone recovered from a site also provides important information about diet and technology, since some tools were made from bones. Archaeologists learn what kinds of fish, birds and mammals the people were hunting and eating, and they can find out about butchering and cooking techniques by identifying cut marks and burning. All of these food remains help archaeologists describe the subsistence of people in their local environments.

On the basis of such reconstructions, archaeologists have a fairly detailed picture of evolving life during this period. Plants were important: acorns and other nuts as well as wild fruits contributed substantially to the diet. Other plants were used for medicines and textiles. One of the most commonly used plants was cattail, the leaves of which were used for weaving floor mats. People spent considerable effort hunting and fishing. Elk, moose, white-tailed deer and the occasional bear were essential large-game resources, yielding large quantities of meat, hides and bone for making tools. They also harvested small mammals, however, by trapping them to reduce the effort involved. Some animals, such as raccoon, beaver and muskrat, were hunted more for their pelts than for food, in which case fall hunting was preferred to ensure that the pelts were in prime condition.

The harvesting calendar would not have been complete without the seasonal catches of fish from Lake Ontario and its rivers. While peo-

mouth bass, yellow perch, walleye, sauger and suckers. In the fall and early winter, a fisher could take lake whitefish and cisco in the shallows, while burbot would follow them in late winter. Year-round residents of the inland waters included lake sturgeon, channel catfish, smallmouth bass, yellow perch and freshwater drum, and in shallow, weedy bays, long-nose gar, bullhead, bowfin, northern pike, muskellunge, walleye and sauger.

Excavations of regional sites have also given archaeologists important insights into long-distance trade and elaborate mortuary ceremonies shared with distant groups throughout northeastern North America. By approximately 3,000 years ago, many of the stone tools, and especially those made from ground stone, had both social and symbolic functions. Many of these objects were made of banded slate and were carved and

ple fished throughout the year, they would have much larger catches during the spawning runs in spring and fall. Indeed, certain deep-water species were available only when they came into shallow waters to spawn. In the spring, the shallows attracted spawning white bass, small-

ground to resemble animals. While they may have had day-to-day uses, such as weights for spear-throwing devices, they also had a sacred meaning, since they were included in burials. Regardless of the context in which they were used or found, they rival any of the art produced anywhere in the world.

This is a replica of a device that was found at an unrecorded southern Ontario site and used to propel spears with greater velocity and accuracy.

EXPANSION, INNOVATION AND INTERACTION (1000 B.C. – A.D. 500)

For the next 1,500 years the strategies people used in different seasons to acquire food varied little from those of previous populations. It was during this period, however, that ceramic vessels, used for cooking and storage of water, were introduced into Ontario from the southeastern

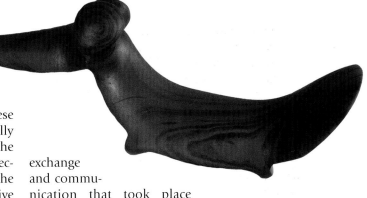

United States. After this, the shards from broken ceramic pots are often found on archaeological sites, along with flake debris created during flintknapping. The craftswomen who made these vessels did not use a potter's wheel, but skillfully coiled and pinched the clay to the form of the pots and then smoothed them and applied decoration to the inside and outside surfaces of the upper rims. Archaeologists use the decorative motifs and decorating techniques to identify the social and political networks to which the potters belonged and to date the site on which they are found. Although useful for archaeologists, these ceramics do not seem to have profoundly changed the hunter-gatherer lifestyle.

Despite the fact that there had not been a large-scale migration of people into the region, populations were growing. Many small regional bands across the southern Ontario landscape probably had a combined population in the thousands. Indeed, based on the archaeological record of sites along major river systems and around inland lakes, archaeologists have estimated the population of southern Ontario to have reached 10,000 people by the turn of the sixth century A.D. Each of the rivers flowing into Lake Ontario through and around the Toronto area may have supported a regional band of 500 people.

Since the bands were largely autonomous, it should not be surprising that groups differed considerably in the design of the stone tools, ceramic pots and other items they used every day. Yet there were also similarities in the decoration of their pottery. Researchers believe these similarities were a result of individual bands participating in two or three larger social networks in southern Ontario.

Archaeologists have discussed the kinds of exchange and communication that took place among neighbouring and distant bands, based on pot fragments and other artifacts. Some archaeologists have argued that the stylistic similarities in ceramic pots of this time resulted from the symbols shared by neighbouring and distant communities — that groups sought such shared styles and symbols to reinforce membership in an expanding network of social relations.

Top: This 2,500-year-old artifact was found at an unrecorded southern Ontario site. Made of banded slate, it is called a birdstone and may have functioned as a weight or handle for a spear-throwing device. Similar objects have been found in the Toronto area.
Bottom: This beautiful beaver effigy, also found in southern Ontario and similar to specimens found in Toronto, was carved and ground from banded slate. Created between two and three thousand years ago, it is an example of some of the most beautiful stone art created in northeastern North America.

In this way, the most frequently expressed artifact styles may have symbolized the most important affiliations of a group, making it easier to identify membership, since these cues were readily apparent to others. The recovery of narrow blades made from Flint Ridge chalcedony (a type of stone) from Ohio, for example, on a site in Mississauga, immediately west of today's city of Toronto, may signify that band's identification with a larger Great Lakes–wide religious belief system that originated in the Mississippi Valley.

There is further evidence across southern Ontario that local bands were increasingly interacting with distant groups, especially sharing burial rituals. It was common 2,500 to 3,000 years ago throughout northeastern North America for people to apply symbolically important red ochre (ground iron hematite) to human remains and the objects placed in their graves. Moreover, scholars have looked at the kinds of objects placed in graves and their variety — for example, beads made of native copper mined at the western end of Lake Superior — and concluded that, since members of the community outside of the immediate family of the deceased provided mortuary offerings, there was a broadening of peoples' social relationships. These items were included in increasingly sophisticated burial ceremonies that sometimes involved the construction of burial mounds. Although bands were competing for resources, one of the first continental free trade zones in North America was flourishing. In Toronto, an elaborate three-thousand-year-old burial site was discovered in the early twentieth century, near Grenadier Pond in High

Left: There was a significant trade in native copper throughout northeastern North America. Copper was mined along the shore of Lake Superior and cold-hammered into sheets that were then cut and formed into objects such as awls, beads and axes. This pan-pipe was found near Port Elgin.

Park, on the lower reaches of the Humber River.

The collections from the Eglinton Flats area and one other nearby site also contain numerous spear points that date to the period from 1,000 to 400 B.C. Since five of the artifacts in the Eglinton Flats collection, which is now housed in the York Historical Museum, are from this time period, those particular specimens probably came from one specific site within the Eglinton Flats area. A survey has determined that intact archaeological deposits may yet be found in the extensive woodlands on the east side of the river. The nearby site is situated in an apartment garden plot located within a relatively undisturbed hydro right-of-way also within the Humber Valley; surprisingly, archaeological deposits sometimes survive in otherwise heavily developed residential and industrial areas.

THE SHIFT TO GROWING FOOD (A.D. 500–1300)

Horticulture profoundly changed the lives of pre-contact Aboriginal peoples in Ontario. Maize was introduced into southern Ontario about 1,600 years ago. While people had been collecting and perhaps even tending plants for food and other uses for thousands of years, plant care was incidental to hunting and other foraging activity, which required a seasonally mobile way of life. People who were on the move could not tend plants for more than a few days or weeks at a time. If they planted or otherwise encouraged the growth of certain plants at a spring-occupied site, they would only do so in the hope of reaping a harvest upon their return at a later time of

Top: This painting by Shelley Huson depicts how mounds were created over dozens of years by community members bringing baskets of soil to the construction site.
Left: This mound in northern Ontario is one of the few surviving examples.

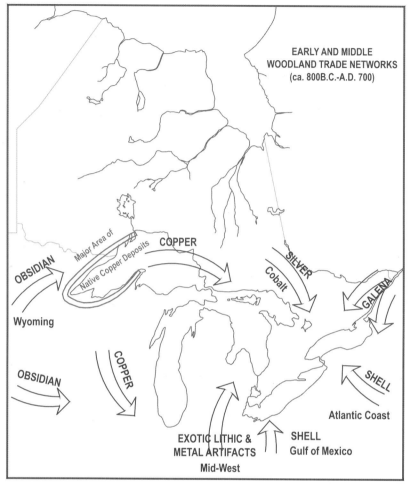

EARLY AND MIDDLE
WOODLAND TRADE NETWORKS
(ca. 800B.C.-A.D. 700)

OBSIDIAN

Wyoming

Major Area of Native Copper Deposits

COPPER

SILVER

Cobalt

GALENA

OBSIDIAN

COPPER

SHELL

Atlantic Coast

EXOTIC LITHIC &
METAL ARTIFACTS

SHELL
Gulf of Mexico

Mid-West

Aboriginal populations were involved in continental trade thousands of years ago — truly the first free-trade zone.

since by A.D. 1300 it often comprised more than half the people's diet. Like squash, it had been domesticated in Mesoamerica several thousand years earlier, although it had taken somewhat longer to adapt to more northerly environments.

The commitment to producing food through agriculture involved abandoning the group mobility that had characterized Aboriginal life for millennia. Instead, people established base settlements and cleared land around them for crops, while sending out hunting, fishing and gathering parties to satellite camps to harvest other naturally occurring resources. While the remains of several sites dating to this period have been found in Greater Toronto Area municipalities, too little has been exposed to learn much about them. From work on places of a similar age in other parts of southern Ontario, however, we know that settlements contained a small number of elliptically shaped houses encircled by a flimsy fence or single-row palisade, likely a windbreak.

The shift from hunting and gathering to agriculture resulted in other changes in addition to a different residential pattern. Over time, a new

the year. While such plants might have been a supplement to their diet, they were not a substantial or reliable source of food.

But all of this changed. Exactly when each of the domesticated plants appeared in the lower Great Lakes region is unclear, but the full suite of Aboriginal cultigens (maize, beans, squash, sunflower and tobacco) was in place 1,200 years ago. Maize was the focus of this subsistence revolution,

Above: Corn was grown in small mounds with squash and beans in the fields surrounding villages.
Right: Carbonized corn cobs of the variety grown by the ancestral Huron and found near Stouffville. The cobs were only five to six inches in length and most had eight rows.

kinship system, or "family tree," emerged which traced descent through the mother's rather than the father's side. This was a profound conceptual change. In band- and tribal-level societies such as these, kinship was the basis for the entire social and political system, and in emerging agricultural societies these systems came to be linked to maternal lineages and clans. Why did the lineages change from paternal to maternal? Scholars have attributed it to the development of separate activity patterns in the new arrangement, whereby women remained in or near villages most of the year to plant, tend and harvest crops, while men were frequently absent on other business. Perhaps it seemed more efficient and less stressful to base the household on a group of women who were closely related and were used to co-operating with one another in carrying out their day-to-day activities. This factor, along with the decreasing importance of hunting and fishing groups, appears to have led men to live with their wives' families, which in turn led to the change in their descent system. The development of the Iroquoian longhouse, a communal residence, during the subsequent period, was related to these earlier changes in social structure.

Some archaeologists argue that it was during this period that Iroquoian-speaking peoples first entered the Great Lakes region, bringing with them a horticultural way of life, with longhouses and maternal lineages. Others believe that they arrived before these developments, bringing ceramics or one of the new styles of spear points that so often swept the region. While the exact timing and catalysts for these changes are unknown, the region had clearly been occupied for thousands of years by proto-Algonkian speakers and their ancestors when Iroquoian-speaking peoples appeared in the lower

This recreation of an Iroquoian house and village at the Longwoods Road Conservation Area near London, Ontario, is representative of the structures that would have appeared in the Toronto area.

Great Lakes region. The people who lived along the central north shore of Lake Ontario were the ancestors of the Neutral, Huron and Petun, while to the south of Lake Ontario, in what is now central New York State, ancestral Iroquoians became the Five Nation Iroquois (Seneca, Cayuga, Onondaga, Oneida and Mohawk). All of these groups were Iroquoian-speaking, and while there were most certainly interactions between them, the Five Nation Iroquois did not inhabit the Toronto area until the mid- to late-seventeenth century.

VILLAGE LIFE (A.D. 1300–1600)

By the beginning of the fourteenth century, and due to the increasing reliance on horticulture, most Iroquoian-speaking people inhabited large fortified villages throughout southern Ontario, including the central north shore of Lake Ontario, within the Humber, Don and Rouge drainage systems. Archaeologists were able to investigate many of these sites, even though many others were destroyed by nineteenth- and twentieth-century urban development. Still, the richness of the archaeological record of this period far surpasses that of previous times, allowing for a better understanding of agricultural village ways of life.

Moreover, new villages are discovered and excavated regularly. The Alexandra site, to take just one case in point, is a fourteenth-century ancestral Huron village discovered in the summer of 2000, during a routine pre-development archaeological assessment along Highland Creek in northeastern Toronto. The site was over two hectares in size and was completely excavated in 2000 and 2001, yielding evidence of 17 longhouse structures, more than 600 subsurface cultural features and approximately 19,000 artifacts.

While the archaeological records of Highland Creek and other river valleys are poorly known, archaeologists have been able to reconstruct century-long settlement sequences for one or perhaps two ancestral Huron communities in the Humber Valley between A.D. 1400 and 1600: one in the middle Humber–Black Creek drainage area and the other at the headwaters of the Humber.

The best-known site of the middle Humber sequence is the Parsons site, a large, late-fifteenth-century ancestral Huron village near the campus of York University, and a subject of both avocational and professional investigations. In the late 1980s, archaeologists carrying out pre-development excavations at the site found parts of ten house structures, several large refuse heaps known as middens and an extensive palisade. Since Parsons is almost twice the size of earlier villages, there may have been two or more earlier sites that amalgamated to form this larger settlement, perhaps in response to growing conflict. We know there was conflict of some form, because of the elaborate defensive systems and scattered human bone on Parsons and on a number of other nearby sites. The early-fifteenth-century Black Creek site, situated on a low terrace of the Black Creek floodplain, is thought to have been one of the immediate predecessor sites to the Parsons community. Professor Norman Emerson of the University of Toronto carried out limited excavations at the site in 1948, and found evidence of a palisaded community, perhaps two hectares in size. An unusual double palisade was discovered along the west side of the site, beside the creek. One row was placed at the base of the terrace, while the other was embedded halfway up the slope. Excavators observed a similar pattern at the Parsons site,

The interior of a recreated Iroquoian longhouse at Longwoods Road Conservation Area. The inside would have been smoky and dark, with corn and other foodstuffs hanging from the rafters, and quite crowded in the winter, with families sharing work and living space.

with one row at the top of slope and the other halfway down, suggesting that the same architectural team designed the palisades of both sites.

The fourteenth-century predecessor villages for this community sequence were likely located along the lower Humber, close to Lake Ontario. These sites, along with sites on the lower reaches of other rivers in the Toronto area, were destroyed by land development before they could be documented by archaeologists.

There was a similar but much later blending

This photograph, from the Mantle site near Stouffville, shows archaeologists working at an excavation where a multiple-row palisade was uncovered. Top right: Shell and glass trade beads similar to these found at Fort Erie have been found at Toronto sites. Most of the glass beads were manufactured near Venice and introduced by Europeans to Aboriginal peoples.

of local villages in the upper reaches of the Humber Valley. Scholars do not know whether the two sequences were related. The Boyd site, situated on the East Humber River near Woodbridge, extends over an area of one hectare. It may have been occupied at the same time as the McKenzie–Woodbridge site, a larger, two-hectare village about three kilometres downstream from Boyd. Professor Emerson excavated portions of seventeen longhouses and a palisade at McKenzie–Woodbridge. Later excavations during the 1970s and 1980s revealed

additional structures. Aboriginal people occupied both communities during the mid- to late sixteenth century, when European goods became available to them, as to other Aboriginal people in southern Ontario, through trade.

The Seed–Barker site, with an area of about two hectares, is situated on a plateau overlooking the East Humber River. The presence of trade goods dates it to the second half of the sixteenth century. Here, archaeologists uncovered a multiple-row palisade and parts of fourteen longhouses. One of the longhouses contained an architectural feature characteristic of contact-period Neutral longhouses, even though the site was more likely occupied by ancestral Huron. At the time of European exploration, the Neutral were located around the west end of Lake Ontario and in the Niagara Peninsula, although their influence is evident at a number of other regional sites, including this one. The discovery of planks related to longhouse benches at Seed–Barker suggests that a Neutral house builder was there, away from his homeland.

The Skandatut site is a three-to-four-hectare ancestral Huron village, situated on a steep-sided promontory overlooking the east branch of the Humber River, approximately one kilometre north of Seed–Barker. The artifacts recovered from a surface collection include over twenty-five ground stone axes and close to a dozen chert arrow points (one of them manufactured from Knife River flint from South Dakota), glass trade beads and copper scrap. The site probably dates to 1580–1600, and represents the latest occupation in the upper Humber River sequence. The site is also located close to the Kleinburg Ossuary, which dates to the same period. The ossuary, excavated in 1970 was a deep pit, 4.2 metres in diameter and 1 metre deep, and it contained the remains of 561 individuals who had died, probably during the occupation of Skandatut village. At the time the ossuary was formed, the remains of people who had been buried previously within or next to the village were disinterred, moved to the pit and mixed together to create a community of the dead. The grave goods buried with the deposit include artifacts of a similar age; some of these are bone and ceramic objects, early-style iron trade axes, an iron kettle, shell beads, native copper beads and large glass trade beads. The Huron–Wendat council in Wendake, Quebec, is currently engaged in efforts to ensure that the site and associated ossuary are permanently protected and commemorated.

There is far less archaeological evidence for Aboriginal communities in the Don drainage system. Early chroniclers of modern Toronto, however, wrote that evidence of Aboriginal encampments had been found frequently along the banks of the Don, especially on the flats near Riverdale Park.

This a rather fanciful depiction of an ancestral Huron Feast of the Dead held when the community reburied all of those who had died during the occupation of their village. Their remains were collected and wrapped in skins and placed in a large communal pit called an ossuary.

These encampments and other sites were investigated by David Boyle in the late nineteenth century. Boyle was a self-taught archaeologist and former school principal who went on to fill the position of curator at the Ontario Provincial

This small ancestral Huron ossuary, containing the remains of 87 people, was found near Leslie Street and Highway 401. Aboriginal leaders have viewed the disturbance to this sacred site as an immense act of disrespect that could have been avoided by proper planning in advance of development.

Museum from 1896 to 1911; its collections later became part of the Royal Ontario Museum. His provincial *Annual Archaeological Reports*, which helped to lay the foundation for Canadian scientific archaeology, are still an essential reference for Ontario archaeologists.

Two large Iroquoian cemeteries, or ossuaries, have also been investigated in the Don River system, one very recently. The Markham Ossuary, located along a tributary of German Mills Creek, which flows into the east branch of the Don River, was discovered in 1881, while workers were building a fence adjacent to Woodbine Avenue. The Toronto *Globe* reported this discovery on Tuesday, May 24, 1881, in an article entitled "'The Red Man': Evidence of His One Time Residency North of Toronto Unearthed."

The discovery captured the attention of Sir Daniel Wilson, one of David Boyle's senior contemporaries. Wilson had come to Canada from Scotland, accepting the post of professor of history and English literature at the new University of Toronto in 1853. By promoting a scientific approach in his extensive writings about pre-contact history, Wilson significantly advanced Canadian archaeology. He collected fifteen skulls from the Markham Ossuary, which were later transferred to the University of Toronto.

In 1997, the late-thirteenth to early-fourteenth-century Moatfield Village and its associated ossuary were discovered. Under the direction of the closest Iroquoian-speaking band, the Six Nations Council of Oshweken, Ontario, the ossuary was completely excavated

Three 700-year-old ceramic pipe bowl effigies, found just west of today's city boundary at the Antrex site. Their flat-cheeked, open-mouthed human forms may be early examples of Iroquois false-face masks.

and the remains re-interred in another location nearby. The site is situated on a small tributary of the Don River about twelve kilometres from Lake Ontario, just south of Highway 401.

Although little of the village was excavated, the remains of over thirty ceramic cooking vessels were found, along with other stone artifacts and large numbers of animal bones. The ossuary, on the periphery of the village, contained at least 87 people, including 6 infants (under one year), 17 young children (one to five years old), 1 juvenile, 5 adolescents and 58 adults. Since these remains are the bones of people who died during the occupancy of the village and were buried in a ceremony at the time of the village's relocation, even a conservative death rate would suggest that several hundred people had inhabited the community.

Establishing villages of this size, or larger, would require planning and a great deal of hard work. The site area and its surrounding agricultural fields would have to be cleared of hardwood forest, mostly maple and beech. Tens of thousands of the felled saplings would be needed to build palisades, houses and other structures. While the inhabitants of the village relied on many different plant and animal species to meet their subsistence needs, the women of the village would have tended hundreds of hectares of maize crops around the village. During the growing season, parties of women and children might have left the village to live in small cabins built in the fields in order to be closer to their crops.

One can determine how much various communities relied on maize in their diet in a number of ways. Charred maize cobs and individual kernels found in pits can sometimes be weighed, and then calculations can be made regarding maize's dietary contribution. A more reliable indicator can be found in the skeletal remains of people. At the Moatfield site, the Six Nations Council permitted analysis of human bone. Consequently, scholars learned a great deal about the diet of fourteenth-century Aboriginal people in the Toronto area. Since maize is a subtropical grass from the highlands

Top: A modern day depiction of an Aboriginal community and its way of life at the Longwoods Road Conservation Area. Bottom: Animal skins were used to clothe people, and bone and antler were used to manufacture beads and other items of adornment.

of Mexico, it leaves a different chemical signature in the bones of people who eat it than any of the other plants in the Great Lakes region. The carbon isotope data from Moatfield suggest that the site inhabitants who died after age fifty had a dietary maize component of 54 percent during their growing years, whereas it reached 70 percent for those aged twenty to twenty-nine when they died. These figures suggest that the need to produce more maize may have become more pressing in some thirteenth- or fourteenth-century communities, even within as short a period as one generation. Tooth decay and periodontal disease in the dental record also attest to increasing reliance on maize, which the Moatfield people probably prepared as sticky gruel, contributing to its effect on teeth. These effects have been documented in the dentitions of subsequent Iroquoian-speaking populations as well.

Despite this reliance on domesticated and naturally occurring plant foods, animal protein was also a crucial part of the diet. Dogs, the only animals to be domesticated by the Aboriginal peoples of southern Ontario, served both as companions and as food in times of scarcity. Hunting and fishing were also important, since people needed animal hides and pelts for clothing, and they manufactured tools with the bones. They likely took most game and fish during the autumn, when they would have mounted large expeditions in order to hunt white-tailed deer and procure spawning fish species.

The large proportion of fish among the animal remains at Moatfield, along with turtles, waterfowl and a variety of both land and water mammals, indicates how important the resources of the lower Don River were for the site inhabitants. In addition to American eel, one group of fish comprising Atlantic salmon, lake whitefish and lake trout played a significant role

Ceramic vessels such as this 500-year-old pot found near Stouffville are found where they were left by the village occupants, likely at the place where the vessel broke. In these instances, it is possible to reconstruct the complete vessel.

in their diet. Indeed, along with pickerel, these species, all of which are high in the food chain, also left a chemical signature in the bones of the village occupants, in the form of high nitrogen isotope values. For those communities situated within fifteen kilometres of the lakeshore, lake fish appear to have provided the nutritional balance to a maize-dominated diet. Similar data from other later communities in the region, situated more than fifteen kilometres from the lakeshore, suggest that deer and other mammals were eaten to achieve that balance.

In addition to the rich archaeological record of this period, scholars often use the written descriptions of Huron life left by the French explorers and missionaries of the seventeenth century to help explain earlier village life. The Huron Confederacy is one of the most extensively

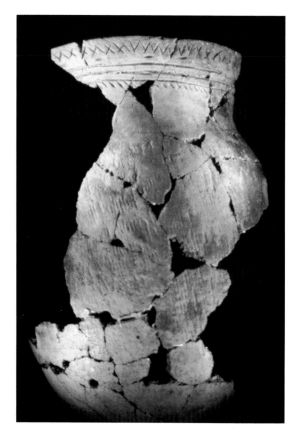

Left: Women were responsible for making many household items such as ceramic pots. Pots vary in shape, with ones from earlier periods having a more elongated form. This pot was found just west of Toronto. Top: This small pot, found in Toronto, was likely made by a child learning the craft from her elders.

documented Aboriginal political organizations in the archival record of seventeenth-century North American exploration. According to these accounts, daily tasks were rigidly organized according to gender. The men of the village were responsible for clearing the agricultural fields and building the village, as well as for hunting, fishing, flintknapping, trading and conducting diplomatic relations with other communities. Women were responsible for growing plants used for food and other purposes and for manufacturing many items, including bone tools and ceramic pots.

To construct the longhouses in which the Huron lived, they selected light, durable and easily worked softwood saplings and cut them so

that they could lash together a series of poles and bend them over a box frame into the shape of an arbour. They removed the bark from larger trees and used it to cover the exterior of the longhouses. Doors were normally located at the house ends or occasionally along the side walls and, in theory, holes in the roof allowed smoke from the hearth fires to escape. Huron health probably suffered, however, as a result of spending too much time in smoke-filled longhouses. Indeed, respiratory infections appear to have been a common problem. The climate of southern Ontario ensured that every year people would spend substantial periods indoors, where smoky air, with age, irritated their facial sinuses. At the Moatfield site, sixty percent of adults of both sexes showed chronic sinusitis. At least four adults, even showed changes to bones of the spine consistent with long-standing tuberculosis. These respiratory issues are consistent with exposure to endemic micro-organisms, which likely thrived in the large, deep middens that contained organic refuse and that were located at the ends of longhouses within the palisade. Living with rodents, dogs and considerable numbers of people would have heightened susceptibility to disease, as would the harmful effects of smoke.

The houses varied in length, depending on the number of people who lived in them — each housing a mother and her daughters, or a group of sisters, living together with their husbands and children. Longhouses could also be lengthened or shortened, to accommodate changes in the numbers of people living inside. Two families probably shared each of the hearths that were situated along the central corridor of the structure, and sleeping benches lined the inside walls. The house ends were often partitioned to create storage areas for firewood or dried corn, and there were pits throughout the house, serving as storage or refuse receptacles. Through the fifteenth century, certain village households became consistently larger and more variable in membership, compared with others in the same community. These differences in house size were greatest around the turn of the sixteenth century, when some longhouses were repeatedly enlarged to reach lengths of over 120 metres — longer than a football field. Some villages attained a size of over four hectares. The differences may reflect changes in the fortunes and solidarity of dominant lineages within villages, or the movement of families between

This 500-year-old human effigy, found near Stouffville, decorated a ceramic pipe bowl and provides a fascinating glimpse at both the art and the faces of early people who inhabited southern Ontario.

This ceramic pipe bowl effigy, found near Stouffville, is approximately 500 years old. It is striking because the decoration is executed in dots, perhaps a reference to tattooing, a practice that early Europeans recorded among Ontario Aboriginal people.

allied communities. During the sixteenth century, longhouses decreased in size and showed fewer differences in their lengths. These changes in residential patterning likely reflect the increasing importance of clans over lineages. Since clan membership cut across related communities, this aspect of kinship was an important means of integrating villages into tribes. When European explorers and missionaries arrived in Ontario at the beginning of the seventeenth century, Iroquoian-speaking tribes, consisting of one or more villages, were under the direction of various chiefs elected from the principal clans. In turn, the tribes themselves were allied within powerful confederacies.

With the move to year-round-occupied sites

Excavation of a semi-subterranean sweat lodge just north of Toronto. These lodges were large, deep, rectangular pits with ramped entrances at one end. They would have had a frame structure covered with skins or bark. The posts of the frame structures are often documented during excavation. Steam was produced by the participants heating rocks in a nearby hearth, rolling them down the ramp and then dousing them with water.

housing large numbers of people, new social and political structures were needed to regulate village affairs and relations between villages. Increases in village size also had consequences for the social and political organization of the individual communities. Village councils, more formalized community planning, various social groups, such as curing societies, as well as group rituals, such as feasting and community burial, all emerged during this time period, although forerunners of some of these ceremonies are evident in earlier times.

Curing societies are first visible in many of the longhouses in the form of semi-subterranean sweat lodges — a special feature that appeared in late-thirteenth-century villages. They consisted of large, deep, rectangular pits with entrance ramps at one end, extending upwards to ground level.

Archaeologists can identify the bottom of the pit by a thin, flat layer of dark soil mottled with charcoal and ash and containing fire-cracked rock and artifacts. This layer, the living floor, developed through use of the lodge and by the repeated dousing of hot rocks to produce steam. The sweat lodges were overlaid by a frame made of bent saplings, perhaps covered with hides or bark. In view of the changes that thirteenth- and fourteenth-century communities experienced in size, kinship organization and residence patterns, sweat lodges may have served to cement the newly emerging social and political ties among the various members of the village and beyond. Occasionally, an animal skull is found on the living floor of a lodge, perhaps symbolizing clan identity. Elaborate bone tools and pipes

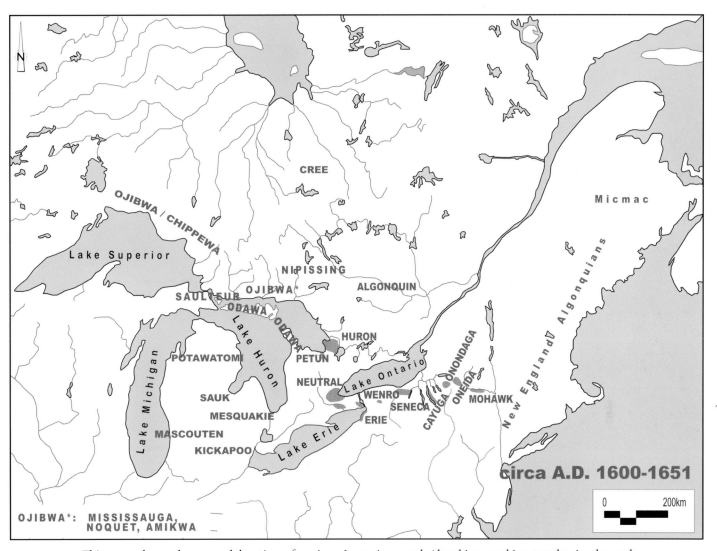

CREE

OJIBWA / CHIPPEWA

Lake Superior

NIPISSING

OJIBWA*

ALGONQUIN

SAULTEUR

ODAWA

OZAWA

HURON

Lake Huron

POTAWATOMI

PETUN

Lake Michigan

NEUTRAL

Lake Ontario

WENRO

ONONDAGA

SAUK

SENECA

ONEIDA

CAYUGA

MOHAWK

MESQUAKIE

ERIE

MASCOUTEN

Lake Erie

KICKAPOO

Micmac

New England Algonquians

circa A.D. 1600-1651

OJIBWA*: MISSISSAUGA,
NOQUET, AMIKWA

0   200km

This map shows the general location of various Iroquoian- and Algonkian-speaking peoples in the early seventeenth century. The grey zones depict where early explorers and priests recorded the principal villages of those nations.

have also been found in these lodges, which sometimes served as places to bury the dead.

While people visited other villages to exchange resources or foodstuffs, they were also motivated to visit for social and political reasons. Regional clusters of villages found by archaeologists may not represent a single community moving from one location to another over time, but rather two or more contemporary communities sharing a hunting territory or some other common resource. In this way, several communities may have belonged to a large social network, in which social links were stronger with neighbouring communities than with more distant groups. Exchange with more distant groups would have brought people exotic goods and ideas, whereas neighbouring communities probably intermarried and forged military alliances and trading relationships, all of which may have prepared people for community amalgamations. Moreover, social ties established by the exchange of marriage partners among the formerly autonomous communities would have helped calm any social and political tensions resulting from the new larger residential populations.

Most if not all the Lake Ontario north shore communities had moved by about 1600, from the lake northward, joining with other groups in present-day Simcoe County (between Lake Simcoe and Georgian Bay) to form the Petun and Huron. While this movement of communities likely took place over many generations, the final impetus was conflict with the Five Nations Iroquois of neighbouring New York State. Intertribal warfare with the Five Nations during the first half of the seventeenth century, worsened by the intrusion of Europeans (and their diseases), ultimately resulted in the collapse and dispersal of the three Ontario Iroquoian-speaking confederacies — the Huron, the Petun and the Neutral — and their Algonkian allies.

The years immediately following their dispersal are poorly documented, although we know that the continuing effects of European diseases, warfare and periods of starvation through the mid- to late-seventeenth century contributed to further population reductions among all Aboriginal peoples. The result was a period of migrations, fission and amalgamation of formerly independent groups, and shifting territories. During this period the Five Nations Iroquois established for the first time a series of settlements in southern Ontario at strategic locations along the trade routes inland from the north shore of Lake Ontario, including two villages in what is now Toronto.

THE SENECA: MID-SEVENTEENTH-CENTURY NEWCOMERS

These new settlements were established by the Seneca near the mouths of the Humber and Rouge rivers, two branches of the Toronto Carrying Place — the canoe-and-portage route that linked Lake Ontario to Georgian Bay and the upper Great Lakes, through Lake Simcoe.

The Humber River settlement was called "Teiaiagon" (now "Baby Point") and is situated on the level summit and slopes of a large promontory overlooking the main channel of the Humber River on the west side of Jane Street and south of St. Clair Avenue. The site was a natural stopping place for canoeists, as they could ford the river at this spot and it was not navigable much farther upstream, even for small canoes.

Historical sources do not often refer to Teiaiagon, although we know that the Recollet missionary and explorer Father Louis Hennepin spent three weeks at the settlement in the late autumn of 1678, while René-Robert Cavelier de La Salle camped at the site in the summer of 1680 and perhaps twice in 1681. The importance of Teiaiagon relates to its location for the fur trade and the fact that it, as well as the contemporary village near the

This map identifies the locations of Seneca and Cayuga villages on the north shore of Lake Ontario in the late seventeenth century, including Teiaiagon, on the Humber River, and Ganatswekwyagon, on the Rouge River.

mouth of the Rouge River, were surrounded by horticultural fields and may have housed hundreds of people in dozens of longhouses.

Archaeologists recorded traces of palisade walls and campfires at Teiaiagon in the late nineteenth century, although the details of this excavation have been lost. When the area was first developed, hundreds of burials were also documented. Despite the fact that archaeologists have recognized for over a century that the archaeolog-

ical resources of Baby Point are significant, the only professional investigations to have been completed were done in the last decade, when natural gas lines were installed for existing houses. Archaeologists encountered the burials of two late-seventeenth-century Seneca women, both in their twenties. Both were moved out of the service trenches in which they were found and reinterred nearby during ceremonies performed by a Six Nations traditional chief.

This moose antler comb, likely worn by a Seneca person, was found at the site of Teiaiagon. It dates to the 1680s and was carved and etched with significant Aboriginal religious symbols.

Both women had been laid to rest along with a number of grave objects meant to accompany them to the next world. The first woman had three brass finger rings, two of which were on her left hand; a small fragmentary brass kettle containing a piece of a fur pelt; and a finely made moose-antler hair comb, carved to depict two human figures wearing European-style clothes flanking an Aboriginal figure. With the other woman was a brass pot containing an ash bowl that in turn contained squash, acorn and grape remains; two iron awls; an iron knife; an iron axe; and another carved and engraved moose-antler comb, which had carved representations of a panther (with a rattlesnake tail), possibly representing Mishipizheu (Mi-shi-pi-zhiw), the chief manitou of the underwater realm. The panther morphs into a bear, another powerful symbol with associations of medicine and resurrection and transition in death from one world to another. The bear morphs into a human figure sitting astride the panther. There are linear, circular and geometric designs etched into the surface of the comb, including modified hourglass, star or thunderbird designs, two circles (one with six and the other with eight radial spokes), criss-crossed lines bordered by two horizontal lines and radiating forked power lines emanating from the panther and bear. The carved, morphing figures, together with the etched lines, form a powerful object of adornment representing the ideology of the Seneca and other seventeenth-century Aboriginal groups. It is replete with references to medicine, either for healing or malevolent purposes, shape-shifting and transformations, and possible journeys and transitions from one world to another.

The other Seneca village in eastern Toronto was called "Ganatsekwyagon" and was known to have been situated near the mouth of the Rouge River. The first European use of the site was as a mission established by the Sulpician Fathers from 1669 to 1671 under François d'Urfé. The missionary François de Salignac de la Motte-Fénélon spent the winter of 1669–70 at Ganatsekwyagon with d'Urfé — the first documented residence of non-Aboriginal peoples in the Toronto region. On the basis of archaeological evidence, Parks Canada has designated a site known as Bead Hill as a National Historic Site commemorating the former location of "Ganatsekwyagon." Archaeologist Dana Poulton conducted test excavations at the site over the course of several years and found over three thousand artifacts, among which were glass trade beads, a 1655 Louis XIV coin, and another Seneca antler comb, which depicts three human figures, one of which appears to be holding a rattle.

Both the Seneca and the earliest Europeans along the present-day Toronto waterfront were there because of the area's strategic importance for accessing and controlling long-established regional economic networks. All these occupations occurred on or near the Lake Ontario shoreline, between the Rouge and Humber rivers, at sites that had both natural landfalls for Great Lakes traffic, and convenient access, by means of the various waterways and overland trails, into the hinterlands. In the end, the first European settlement of Toronto was simply a continuation of patterns that had been in place for thousands of years. In their success, the visitors became so content that they decided to stay.

Chapter 3

COLONIAL TRANSFORMATIONS

Carl Benn

MISSISSAUGA TORONTO, 1701–1793

As the Iroquois colonization of southern Ontario came to an end around 1700, Algonkian-speakers moved south from the Canadian Shield and replaced the Iroquois in Toronto and neighbouring regions. The newcomers were associated closely with the Ojibways (or Anishnaubeg), and became known to Europeans as the Mississaugas. In the 1690s they established one of their settlements near the former Seneca village of Teiaiagon on the Humber River, which sat astride the most impor-

tant route of the ancient Toronto Passage, connecting Lake Ontario via waterways and trails to Georgian Bay and the world beyond in the north. It also lay beside the Humber's southerly fording spot on the east-west trail that ran along the north shore of Lake Ontario.

These newcomers, according to a text preserved in the *New York Colonial Documents* (Vol. 4, p. 694) told the Iroquois in the winter of 1699–1700 that they intended to "plant a tree of peace and open a path for all people." One of their objectives was to form an alliance with the

This 1807 print depicts a hunting and fishing camp of the kind the Mississaugas set up during their seasonal round of subsistence activities. Unlike the Iroquois, the Mississaugas — whose population was not large — did little farming.

This trade axe from the fur trade era is typical of the tools that Native peoples acquired from Europeans, along with such other goods as weapons, cloth, clothing and ornamental items.

Iroquois and share hunting territories with them. Such a relationship would expand the regions in which they could hunt, gather or fish, as well as enhance their diplomatic strength on the volatile Great Lakes frontier and create mutual obligations with the Iroquois to help each other in times of crisis. Another objective was to link the British trading posts at Albany and Schenectady in New York to the Toronto Passage. This would benefit the Mississaugas by improving the ability of British traders to compete with the French in this region, with the result that Natives would have access to a wider range of European materials at better prices. At the same time it would restrict the influence the French could exercise over them if they were the only suppliers of foreign goods. In effect, the Mississaugas hoped to play the two European powers off against each other to protect their own trade and political interests. In addition, their control of the Humber would allow them to act as intermediaries in trade between the British and the tribes to the north, and to collect presents as demonstrations of respect and friendship from people who wanted to travel along the Toronto Passage through Mississauga territory.

For their part, the Iroquois confederacy (comprising the Mohawk, Oneida, Onondaga, Cayuga and Seneca nations at that time) was satisfied to have an allied nation take their place on the north shores of lakes Ontario and Erie. After having overstretched themselves expanding their territories between the 1650s and the 1670s — including their move into southern Ontario — the Iroquois had been forced to contract in the Ohio country and elsewhere under military pressure by both hostile tribes and the French. In southern Ontario, however, they do not seem to have been forced out (although some historians have thought so, after attributing Algonkian oral traditions about warfare with Iroquoians to the late 1600s, although these conflicts likely occurred much earlier). Nevertheless, the Iroquois could not hold this region and preferred to create an alliance and share with the Algonkian newcomers. In the 1701 Treaty of Montreal with the French, as well as in contemporary treaties with the British in Albany, Native peoples acknowledged the Aboriginal geo-political relationships that had emerged in the 1690s, while the Iroquois got Europeans to affirm their hunting and other rights in southern Ontario, even though the land now was occupied by others. In subsequent decades they too played the French against the British in order to gain presents, favourable trade and other concessions from the white powers, as well as keep the Europeans out of their own lands in upstate New York.

The French and British were aware of Aboriginal actions and tried to mitigate their consequences for their own benefit, both in time of war against each other (1701–1713, 1744–1748, and 1754–1763) and in the periods of uneasy peace between conflicts. During the first half of the century, Europeans were limited in what they could achieve in the Great Lakes region. Their economic interests — centred on the fur trade rather than on settlement — demanded good relations with the

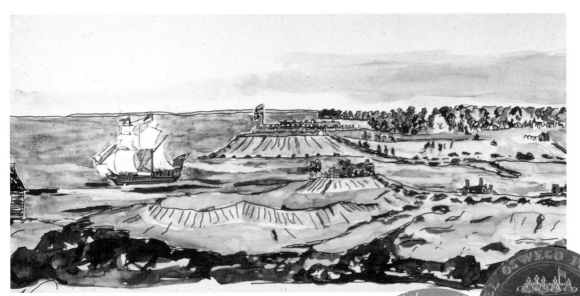

Above: A view of Fort Oswego.
Right: Silver medal struck in 1758 to commemorate the capture of British Fort Oswego in 1756.

indigenous peoples, while their inability to project significant military power into the interior required that they cultivate the Aboriginal population who held the balance of power. Therefore, like the First Nations, the British and French used trade and diplomacy to further their aims. Of the two, the French possessed more knowledge of the region and its tribes, and maintained a larger presence throughout the Great Lakes and beyond. The British reached only as far north as Oswego, on the southeastern shore of Lake Ontario, in 1726, where they built a fort, but did not progress further until the Seven Years' War in the 1750s.

The French had known about the Toronto Passage from the early 1600s and had set up camps to trade along the route from time to time, but maintained a permanent presence in Toronto only in the 1720s and again in the 1750s. In 1720, they built a small *Magasin royal* near its south end on the Humber River to trade and to promote good relations with both the Mississaugas and the tribes from farther north that used this route. At the same time, they established other posts, including one on the Niagara River. They wanted to have separate posts in Toronto and Niagara in order to weaken the Iroquois–Mississauga alliance and expand French influence with these peoples. However, the *Magasin* at Toronto seems to have failed financially, in part because of competition from the British in Oswego after 1726, as well as from illegal, independent French traders, who

Fort Niagara at the mouth of the Niagara River in modern Youngstown, New York, was the main French post in the Lake Ontario region during the French Regime.

undercut the post's commercial viability. Consequently, the *Magasin royal* was abandoned by 1730.

During the War of Austrian Succession (1744 to 1748 in North America), the Mississaugas continued to trade with the British at Oswego, and some even allied with them, although others fought alongside the French. (Members of a tribe might join opposing sides in the imperial rivalries, but they rarely fought against their relatives.) After the return of peace, the French built a small post on the Humber in the spring and summer of 1750 to intercept Oswego-bound furs from the Toronto Passage and cultivate better relations with the Natives. Almost immediately, the volume of trade exceeded expectations, and the French found they could not store enough goods at the site. At the same time, the tribespeople intimated that they might abandon Oswego if this new post could meet

their needs. Therefore, the French replaced it with a larger one, which also would be more defensible should the Natives decide to loot the increased quantities of supplies that would be stored there. In September 1750, construction began on Fort Rouillé (or Fort Toronto), a few kilometres east of the Humber on the shore of Lake Ontario. More or less completed by the spring of 1751, it was a modest establishment, normally housing a garrison of only ten to fifteen people, and served as an outstation of the larger post of Fort Niagara (in modern Youngstown, New York).

Despite its humble size, Fort Rouillé was a successful trading post, although much of its business came at the expense of Niagara and other French posts rather than Oswego, partly because of Oswego's convenient location, but also because a large proportion of French goods were not competitive in price or quality with those of the British. After the Seven Years' War broke out in North America in 1754, Fort Rouillé demonstrated its worth when Mississaugas who had been frequenting the post agreed to participate in a strike against Oswego in 1756. It fell after a short siege. Yet tensions continued, and in 1757 ninety hostile Natives surrounded Fort Rouillé and threatened to kill its eleven-man garrison. Two people from the fort escaped by canoe to seek help at Fort Niagara, whose commandant dispatched sixty-three soldiers

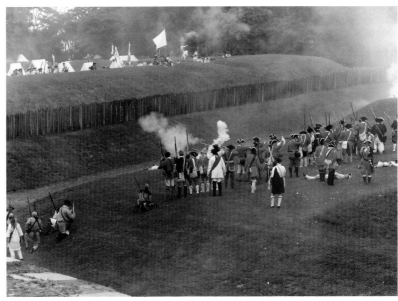

A re-enactment of the English attack on Fort Niagara.

across the lake in two whaleboats to rescue the garrison at Toronto. The appearance of the armed boats carrying the soldiers brought a quick and non-violent end to the confrontation. Ironically, the warriors were en route to fight the British on the Lake Champlain front, but had planned to pillage the stores at Toronto on their way. They tried to excuse their behaviour with various reasons, such as rumours that the French had sent troops to North America to kill them. However, we have only French records for this incident, and given what we know about the characteristics of Native-white relations on the Great Lakes frontier, we might be forgiven for wondering if the French perhaps had offended the Natives or had shown a lack of the generosity expected of friends and allies by not giving the warriors enough supplies and presents for the Lake Champlain expedition, and thus had brought the crisis on themselves.

In 1758, the British re-occupied Oswego and captured Fort Frontenac (in modern Kingston), along with French vessels on Lake Ontario and stores intended for the fur trade. In the wake of these events, the garrison of the increasingly vulnerable and isolated Fort Rouillé received instructions to burn their post and retire to Fort Niagara, the main French post in the region, if the British were to appear. Then, in 1759, the commandant of Fort Rouillé was told that, if Niagara were to be threatened, he was to recruit as many Mississaugas as he could and send them to reinforce the larger fort. In July 1759, the British besieged Niagara and destroyed a relief force dispatched from the Ohio country. After a nineteen-day siege, Fort Niagara surrendered. Two days later, the British sent about thirty soldiers across Lake Ontario to reconnoitre Fort Rouillé. However, its French garrison had assumed that Niagara had fallen once they no longer could hear artillery fire from across the lake, so they already had burned and abandoned

Fort Rouillé is remembered with a monument at the west end of the Exhibition Grounds, constructed in the 1880s and shown here in a c.1910 photograph. Remains of the French post were visible until 1878 when the site was graded for fair grounds.

the post and retreated towards Montreal. After inspecting the ruins, the redcoats returned to Niagara, accompanied by a local Mississauga chief, Tequakareigh, who previously had fought alongside the French but who now sought to negotiate a diplomatic, military and trade alliance with the British.

Among other disasters to strike the French in 1759, the greatest was the fall of Quebec in September. Then, in 1760, Montreal capitulated, and in the 1763 Treaty of Paris, New France (including Toronto) was transferred to British sovereignty. At the time of this great change, Mississauga–British relations suffered from deep stresses, in part because of aggressive behaviour by traders who came to the Toronto Passage and exploited the Natives with rum, and in part because British officials, no longer competing with the French for Aboriginal affections, dramatically reduced the presents and attention they gave the tribespeople and began to treat them less as allies and more as subjects. As a result of these events, and inspired by a growing hostility to the new order throughout the Great Lakes (made worse by a post-war flood of settlers into Native lands to the south), some of the Toronto-region Mississaugas joined the rising of 1763–1764, known popularly as the Pontiac War. However, the conflict came to an end as the British and First Nations worked out a tense but viable relationship with each other. With the end of the crisis, the Mississaugas continued to live in southern Ontario as before, and various people of Native and white origin traded in and around the Toronto Passage.

To the south, many colonists rose up against imperial rule in the American Revolution of 1775–1783. During the conflict, the Crown recruited warriors to shore up the loyalist cause, including Mississaugas from Toronto, who fought on the lower Great Lakes front. After the rebel victory, Britain recognized the independence of the new United States in 1783 and negotiated the creation of the Canadian-American border. A significant number of loyalists, as well as Natives from the south side of the Great Lakes, moved north to remain within British territory. In the war's aftermath, people began to examine Toronto's potential, both to expand the fur trade business in the region to replace the trade in the south, and as a site for settlement. Consequently, they began to petition for land here. As it turned out, the passage proved to possess only a limited potential for growth in the fur trade because most traders who operated in the north preferred to travel northwest from Montreal up the Ottawa River and across the other waterways that had been used in earlier days, rather than use the Toronto route.

With this developing interest, the Crown purchased Toronto from the Mississaugas on September 23, 1787, for £1,700 in cash and goods. (The boundaries, however, were not understood clearly, and a subsequent treaty in 1805 clarified the details of the purchase.) For their part, the Mississaugas were willing to sell land for three reasons. First, the small amount of settlement that had occurred up to that point had chased away game and ruined fisheries, which made the region less viable for their own subsistence needs. Second, they wanted to affirm their friendship with the British in hopes that their interests might be respected as the world changed around them. Finally, they often felt they had no choice, because government pressure to alienate land could be intense and even threatening. (Nevertheless, First Nations people did not "disappear," and in the twenty-first century there are more Aboriginal inhabitants in Toronto than at any previous time in history.)

Little happened after the "Toronto Purchase," aside from the arrival of a handful of Loyalists to join the small number of traders (mainly French-Canadians) in the Toronto region; most Loyalists settled along the Detroit, Niagara and St.

John Graves Simcoe, the man who founded urban Toronto in 1793 during a period of Anglo-American tension, is depicted here in a 1791 portrait wearing the uniform of the Queen's Rangers.

Lawrence rivers or towards the eastern end of Lake Ontario. These newcomers, with their interest in clearing land and establishing farms, heralded the end of the white-Native middle ground of the fur trade era. It would be replaced by an agricultural-commercial economy that would find it hard to integrate or respect Aboriginal interests in the decades that followed. As the loyalist society began to take shape, the British government divided the "old" Province of Quebec (which then included southern Ontario) into two new provinces in 1791, Upper and Lower Canada, and the seat of government for the loyalist upper province was set in Niagara.

THE BIRTH OF URBAN TORONTO, 1793–1815

Probably Toronto would have evolved slowly without much Euro-american settlement for many years, and a large city that would come to dominate the province might never have developed here, except that in 1793 a military crisis forced the early creation of an urban place and set in motion forces that would give it important advantages over other centres in Upper Canada. In that year John Graves Simcoe, the province's lieutenant-governor, decided to move the provincial capital, at least temporarily, to Toronto, and ordered fortifications to be built to guard the entrance to the harbour.

This watercolour by Elizabeth Simcoe shows the Queen's Rangers' camp at Fort York, July 30, 1793, when "urban" Toronto was only ten days old.

hostilities. Faced with a worsening crisis, Simcoe decided to establish a naval base at Toronto immediately and move his capital there from the exposed border town of Niagara, until calm returned and he could place the capital in his preferred location, at modern London, Ontario.

The genesis of Simcoe's decision lay in the Ohio country to the southwest, where the First Nations had continued fighting the United States after the end of the American Revolution in an attempt to preserve their homelands from unwanted white settlement. Although not at war with the United States, the British were allied to the Natives, and even maintained forts on American soil (at Niagara and Detroit, for example) in violation of the peace of 1783, arguing that the new republic had failed to live up to some of its obligations in the treaty. As the Ohio peoples showed remarkable skill in repelling the Americans in the late 1780s and early 1790s, many in the United States clamoured not only for the defeat of the tribes, but for the annexation of British territory as well. Then, in the spring of 1793, word reached the frontier that France had gone to war with Britain. This made a confrontation more likely, because France was an ally of the United States and worked to destabilize the Great Lakes region to Britain's disadvantage. At the same time, other border tensions, such as plans by Vermont filibusters to seize Lower Canada, increased the possibility of

Earlier, Simcoe had developed an ambitious plan to defend the province, intending Toronto to be his main military base, but at that time there was little chance that his grand scheme could have been implemented because of the limited funding available for Canadian defence from Britain, which had greater military priorities elsewhere in the world. However, in light of the looming threat in 1793, the establishment of Toronto became possible, especially when Simcoe jettisoned most of his larger designs to focus on Toronto itself, and acted on his own initiative without waiting for consent from the governor-in-chief of British North America, Guy Carleton, Baron Dorchester. Simcoe surveyed Toronto in May 1793, and then dispatched soldiers of the Queen's Rangers from Niagara in mid-July to begin the construction of Fort York to guard the entrance to Toronto Bay. That act was the birth of urban Toronto. A few weeks later, on August 27, 1793, the lieutenant-governor named his little settlement "York" to honour the Duke of York, son of King George III, although many people liked the old name better and continued to use it. Over the next year

Sempronius Stretton's 1804 watercolour shows the garrison at York. The large building is a blockhouse, a defensible building with bulletproof walls, loopholes for shooting at attackers, and other features to enable troops to defend themselves.

Simcoe built additional defences on the south side of the harbour at Gibraltar Point (near modern Hanlan's Point), and laid out a ten-block town site bordered by today's Front, George, Adelaide and Berkeley streets. To the north, across "Lot Street," now Queen, Simcoe set aside a series of "park lots" that extended to modern Bloor Street to provide substantial estates for senior officials and other worthies, and he assumed that agricultural settlement by people of more humble origins would occur beyond this immediate area. He attracted civilian settlers to supply the goods and services the military needed, built a sawmill on the Humber, and began construction of Yonge Street to improve the capacity of the Toronto Passage to carry troops and supplies to the north by replacing its southern section with a military road because the passage's more southerly waterways were less capacious than in the north.

In Simcoe's mind, York's defensible harbour would allow the British to control Lake Ontario and support military operations on the Niagara Peninsula should it become a battleground. As well, the Toronto Passage would enable troops and supplies to move to the upper lakes (and then south to the Ohio country) should the Americans gain control of Lake Erie and thereby cut the traditional route to the southwest. There were, however, problems with his plan. First, Baron Dorchester thought that Simcoe's priorities were wrong, and that he should concentrate on protecting the St. Lawrence River, Upper Canada's lifeline to the rest of the British Empire. Therefore Dorchester would not authorize funding to make York into a strong provincial bastion. Fortunately the war scare passed, and significant defences were not needed at that time. The Americans defeated the Ohio tribes in 1794, then negotiated a peace treaty with them in 1795; the British and

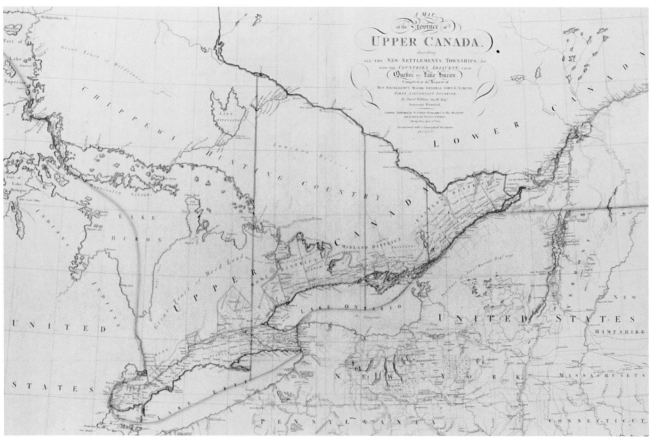

Note how the Toronto Passage connected Lake Ontario to the upper Great Lakes on this 1800 map of Upper Canada and how the Town of York was located at a safer distance from the U.S. border compared to the rival towns of Niagara and Kingston.

Americans signed Jay's Treaty in 1794 to resolve their differences; the Royal Navy captured a ship carrying guns from France that the Vermont filibusters needed for their invasion; and French intrigue in the Great Lakes region never developed into a serious problem.

When Simcoe left Upper Canada in 1796, York was very much a raw backwoods community. There were no roads to connect it to settlements to the east and west, which meant that the village sat cut off from most of the world during the winter months, when the lake routes could not be used. However, Yonge Street opened to the north in 1796. With that event,

the Toronto Passage below the Holland River largely passed into history and the new road took its place as the main route to the interior. In later years, additional roads would render the rest of the old route to Georgian Bay obsolete, but the fundamental value inherent in the Toronto Passage — that of providing access to the interior and a shortcut between the lower and upper Great Lakes — remained in place, and in fact drove much of the new and more expansive road network that supplanted older Native routes. At the same time, the shift away from the Humber River in favour of the sheltered harbour was a turning point in Toronto's history. On the one hand, fear of American invasion, which had not dissipated with Jay's Treaty, suggested that Toronto Bay might yet play an important role in the defence of Upper Canada. On the other hand, the focus on the bay as a port facility signalled the demise of the old fur-trade economy and its replacement with one centred on settlement and the promise of commercial growth to serve the expanding Euro-american society forming in Upper Canada (and even on the Humber, milling, shipbuilding

This 1804 watercolour by Elizabeth Francis Hale shows the waterfront (now Front Street) where the town's leading citizens lived. In the background is a blockhouse, built in 1798 during the war scare with the Mississaugas. Nearby stand the brick parliament buildings, constructed in the years 1796–98.

and the other endeavours of a new economy supplanted older subsistence patterns).

Life was hard in the little settlement in the 1790s. Food was in such short supply at one point in 1796 that the army had to feed the civilian population, and over the two years that followed the townspeople worried that they might be attacked by the Mississaugas after a grim set of small confrontations, most famously the murder of Wabacanine, a chief who had signed the Toronto Purchase, and his wife on the Toronto waterfront in 1796. Fortunately for both sides, the crisis passed without recourse to arms. Later, in 1806, people feared that they might have to abandon the settlement when forest fires raged nearby. Despite these problems, York, as the seat of government and a garrison town, with its northerly road to the good lands of the interior, had achieved a level of security and purpose

that gave it an advantage in competing with its larger rivals of Niagara and Kingston, and by 1799 and 1801 roads connected the town respectively to the west and the east, further solidifying its future. Yet growth was slow. In 1797, aside from the 175 or so soldiers and dependants in the garrison, there were only 241 people in the town itself (with 196 more settlers in the surrounding countryside). In 1812, aside from the garrison, 703 people lived in York.

In June 1812, the United States declared war on Great Britain, and in July American troops invaded Canada. The government of President James Madison had a number of objectives in the war, the greatest being the conquest of Canada, but, by the time peace returned in 1815, the Americans had failed to achieve their goals. Yet, at the outbreak, most people expected the invaders to seize Upper Canada without much

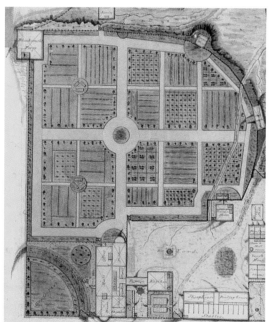

Maryville Lodge was the home of D.W. Smith, one of York's more prominent citizens. Despite the grandness of the house (and its grounds, right), it was not as large or prominent as elite homes in more established centres, and thus was representative of frontier conditions in early York.

difficulty, because the population of the United States outnumbered that of British North Americans by a ratio of fifteen to one. The situation was even worse in Upper Canada, where the majority of people were immigrants from the enemy republic, who had come here after the Loyalists, fundamentally in search of good land, and who might be expected to support an invasion (although they would turn out to be more loyal to the Crown than American optimists and British pessimists had assumed in 1812). Furthermore, with King George's army and navy concentrating their efforts against Napoleon Bonaparte's ambitions to turn the United Kingdom into a French vassal state, there would be few resources available to devote to fighting the Americans until the situation in Europe changed, which many people, including the US government, did not expect would happen before the fall of Canada. Yet in the end, British troops, local militia and their Aboriginal allies turned back the invaders, thereby enabling the nascent

Canadian experiment of building a North American society to continue, rather than end prematurely through violent foreign conquest.

Despite the satisfactory outcome to the War of 1812, the conflict was traumatic for the citizens of York. The town itself was attacked on three occasions. On April 27, 1813, the enemy landed west of the town and fought a six-hour battle against the outnumbered defenders before capturing the provincial capital. Immediately after the battle and the retreat of British troops and Native warriors, the leading citizens of the town surrendered their community to the Americans, who occupied York for six days. Despite agreeing to respect private property and allow the civil government to function without hindrance, the Americans robbed homes and torched the governor's home at Fort York and the provincial parliament buildings at Front and Parliament streets. Those acts led to the retaliatory burning of the White House, Congress and other public buildings when British forces captured

In the battle of York, 2,650 Americans defeated 750 British, Canadians, Mississaugas, and Ojibways in a six-hour battle at a cost of 157 British and 320 Americans killed and wounded. Just before retreating, the British blew up their gunpowder magazine, seen in this c.1815 engraving.

Washington in 1814. The invaders returned to a defenceless York on July 31, 1813, and stayed for two days to burn barracks and other buildings that they had missed in April. Shortly afterwards, the British rebuilt York's defences, and in August 1814 the fortifications were strong enough to repel the US squadron when it again tried to enter Toronto Bay. Outside of these dramatic events, the townspeople spent three years worrying about their future, endured shortages and crippling inflation, and participated in the overall defence of the colony. Some merchants even prospered in the war, earning enormous profits through supplying the needs of the

province's defenders, and in the end, the return of peace in 1815, with Canada remaining within the British Empire, validated the sacrifices and stresses of the previous three years.

A PROVINCIAL CENTRE, 1815–1851

The make-up of York and of the province as a whole changed dramatically after 1815. On the one hand, American immigration essentially dried up. On the other hand, the economic turmoil that followed the British and allied victory over Napoleon, combined with industrialization and modernization in the United Kingdom,

This 1793 watercolour by Elizabeth Simcoe shows John Scadding's home on the Don River.

created severe economic and social stresses that led many people to seek a new life for themselves in Canada. Combined with natural growth, this immigration increased the population of the town from 720 souls at the end of the War of 1812, to 1,600 in 1825, to 5,550 in 1832 — when its population surpassed that of Kingston to make it Upper Canada's largest centre — and then on to 9,250 in 1834, to 14,250 in 1841, and to 31,775 in 1851.

This increase, along with the settlement elsewhere in Upper Canada, transformed Toronto from a frontier town into a significant commercial centre surrounded by a large and growing agricultural hinterland. Economic prosperity came in large part from serving that hinterland, as exemplified by the growth of the town's merchant operations and the founding of institutions such as the Bank of Upper Canada in 1822 and the British American Fire and Life Assurance Company in 1834. Expanding commercial activity, facilitated by the town's port and road networks, intensified relationships and trade with other communities around the Great Lakes and on the St. Lawrence, and turned York into the dominant centre in the Upper Canadian

economy. Improved transportation came when steamboats began to ply the waters of Lake Ontario in 1816 and when the opening of the Erie Canal in the mid-1820s connected Toronto to New York City with greater efficiency through Rochester and Oswego. In 1833 the Welland Canal made transportation around Niagara Falls faster and more economical than before, when goods had to be carried laboriously around the great barrier. There were other, less dramatic, transportation improvements, such as the macadamization of part of Yonge Street in the 1830s, and the development of other roads and canals, but they too made their contributions. Industrial output, however, was modest in Toronto during these years, with few operations expanding beyond workshop enterprises that met local needs, although portents of future growth could be seen as early as the 1830s, with the introduction of steam-driven machinery in some establishments.

As the capital, Toronto attracted both a disproportionate number of government agencies and the provincial elite, whose influence and connections benefited the city, and encouraged organizations with a colony-wide interest to locate here. Two educational institutions became well known: the prep school Upper Canada College, founded in 1830, and the university King's College (chartered in 1827, although it did not open its doors until 1843). In turn, this concentration of governmental, commercial and institutional power gave the community greater influence on provincial society than its rivals could hope to achieve. To cite just two examples of how this played out, the town's Anglican church, originally constructed in 1807 as a modest wooden building, was not considered to be the best parish in the colony at that time.

However, it was enlarged in 1816 to house a growing congregation, and then was replaced by a grand stone structure in 1833, which burned in 1839, to be replaced by another edifice. When completed, this building no longer was a mere parish church, or even the house of worship of the capital's elite, but rather the cathedral of the newly created Diocese of Toronto, which then incorporated all of Upper Canada under the care of its recently consecrated bishop, John Strachan. Another example of cultural growth was the healthy newspaper industry in the town, represented by seven papers in 1834. At the same time, there were real limits on cultural and recreational opportunities, but the city was not without some degree of diversity, running from the houses of ill repute on Lombard Street to Lenten lectures presented at St. James Cathedral on topics such as the history of early Christianity.

By the early 1830s, those responsible for the urbanizing environment found that the laws and taxing powers available to them were inadequate to provide the municipal services, such as sewers, that the growing community needed. A few officials had been elected at town meetings from 1797 onwards to look after minor matters, such as impounding stray animals, while provincially appointed magistrates had levied small local taxes and addressed larger issues in the "Home District" (the larger political division of the province that included York), such as maintaining the peace, supervising taverns and protecting public health. However, these administrative structures were not enough, so the provincial government passed legislation converting the old Town of York into the new City of Toronto on March 6, 1834 — the first incorporated municipality in the colony. Now an elected mayor, aldermen and councilmen attended to the public affairs of Toronto with expanded municipal powers. The city in 1834 consisted of five wards, bounded by Parliament Street on the east,

John Strachan (depicted here in 1827) became prominent during the War of 1812. He was the Anglican rector of York who promoted the British cause, worked to relieve wartime suffering and stood up to the Americans during the occupation of York.

Bathurst on the west, and a point about 365 metres north of Queen Street on the north, plus the city "liberties" beyond, where new wards could be created, and which extended to the Don River and Ashbridge's Bay in the east, Dufferin Street in the west and Bloor Street in the north. The first mayor was the radical politician and newspaper publisher William Lyon Mackenzie.

Although the town grew in population, prosperity and sophistication, the period 1815–1851 was marked by strain and trauma that caused enormous stress and tribulation for its people. For example, economic growth was not even or always progressive: between 1819 and 1822 the people of York lived through a grim period of

William Lyon Mackenzie. Left, reproductions of broadsheets printed on Mackenzie's press.

economic restraint; then in 1825 a downturn in Britain affected Canada, followed by a slow recovery; then in 1837 an international depression hit Toronto hard, negatively affecting prosperity until the beginning of the 1840s. There also was poverty and distress in a society that provided little support for the poor and needy. (However, a poor house opened in 1837, which reflected Torontonians' embrace of larger trends in the Western world, even in the case of something as baleful as treating poverty through

incarceration, a comparatively new phenomenon in the transatlantic world.) As was typical, poverty's symptoms found expression in drunkenness, violence and crime. In general, such relief as was available came through charities, rather than from governments. For example, in one month in 1822, the Society for the Relief of the Sick and Destitute in York looked after twenty-two cases of one or more people drawn from what the town's more respectable citizens considered to be the "deserving poor," comprising

The new parliament buildings constructed 1829–32 on Front Street, as depicted in an 1835 lithograph.

the sick, the old and the infirm, who were unable to support themselves because of conditions beyond their control. In 1832 and 1834, the horror of cholera struck Toronto. It killed 273 people during its first visitation, then took over five hundred more lives on its return two years later. Even in the face of these massive disasters, much of the relief that people received came from charity, as exemplified by John Strachan's Society for the Relief of Widows and Orphans of York, which raised £1,263 during the course of the two plagues, an amount that rivalled the combined expenditures of the provincial and local authorities. Typhus hit the city in 1847–48, and carried off over eleven hundred souls, especially among the immigrants passing through Toronto on their way to what they had hoped would be better lives in Canada. Then, in 1849, cholera came back and stole another 420 lives.

Although less mortal than contagious disease, the most famous crisis of the 1815–1851 era was the Rebellion of 1837, in which William Lyon Mackenzie led an armed mob down Yonge Street on December 5, intent on overthrowing the government, but was repulsed near modern College Street, and then dispersed by loyal Upper Canadians, who counterattacked up Yonge against his headquarters at Montgomery's Tavern (north of modern Eglinton Avenue and Yonge Street) two days later. The rebellion symbolized how polarized and uncompromising the colony's politics had become over the preceding years and represented the desperation felt by many people who had been crushed by the worldwide depression that hit at the same time. It set in motion several years of deep discord, marked by a variety of border raids into Canada (largely undertaken by American sympathizers of the rebel cause). These raids were far more serious than anything Mackenzie attempted and re-awakened the nightmares of 1812–1814 in people's minds, to say nothing of the strains that

A watercolour of curling on the Don River near a mill, 1836, attributed to John Howard.

arose when neighbours pitted themselves against each other with new levels of animosity and belligerence during the crisis.

In attempting to solve the problems that led to rebellion, the British government did away with the old provinces of Upper and Lower Canada in 1841, replacing them with the single United Province of Canada (sub-divided into Canada East and Canada West). The capital of the new colony first met in Kingston, Toronto's old but now smaller rival (although parliament would return to Toronto in 1849–1851 during a period when the capital moved every few years — until Queen Victoria settled on Ottawa in the late 1850s). However, Toronto by 1841 had become

sufficiently large and diverse that its future security was not unduly threatened by that loss, and a rapidly recovering economy more than absorbed the change in the city's government status. The last pre-railway years were marked largely by expanded growth in population, trade, culture and confidence. At the same time, a recognizably modern city began to take shape, due in part to the innovations of the Victorian era, such as the coming of gas home and street lighting in 1842, and the opening of a waterworks in 1843.

Yet, before the coming of the railways, one more significant setback occurred. On the night of April 7, 1849, a great fire swept through part of the downtown, destroying the city blocks

A view of King and York Streets looking east, in a watercolour by John Howard, 1834.

encompassed by Church, George, King and Adelaide streets, with the 1839 St. James Cathedral being its most famous victim. As new buildings on a grander scale rose to replace the lost structures, one particularly representative edifice of mid-century Toronto that took shape was St. Lawrence Hall, at the southwest corner of King and Jarvis streets. Opened in 1851, it was an important public building, combining retail shops, the market in the rear, meeting and assembly rooms, and a ballroom, where Torontonians could enjoy various performances,

St. Lawrence Hall opened in 1851 as the city's primary cultural venue. Built at a time when Toronto experienced an influx of runaway Black slaves from the United States, the hall figured as an important site for anti-slavery meetings and associated events.

hold public meetings and celebrate worthy causes. It was a grand structure for the city — handsome, with a cupola and impressive carved stonework, and it expressed the sophistication and optimism that the people of the city had achieved by mid-century. At the same time, however, it signified Toronto's limits as a pre-railway regional colonial centre, being constructed to follow precedents for similar civic centres in British provincial towns without the population or sophistication to support independent concert halls and other cultural facilities. However, the same year, as we will learn in the next chapter, the railway construction began in the city, and Toronto embarked on a period of stunning and rapid change that overshadowed the already impressive growth that had occurred since 1815.

Chapter 4

THE AGE OF INDUSTRY

Christopher Andreae

In the autumn of 1851, Fort York, representing the august military presence of the British Empire, still guarded the western entrance to Toronto Harbour. In the east, near the mouth of the Don River, stood the Gooderham and Worts Distillery, an industry based on the agricultural economy in the wider Toronto region. Between these two structures stretched the official City of Toronto, largest city in Canada West and some-time colonial capital.

The developed urban area at this point cov-ered the plain back from the harbour as far as the vicinity of College Street. With 30,800 people in 1851, Toronto was more than twice as large as its neighbouring prominent Lake Ontario ports in Hamilton (14,100) and Kingston (11,600). Yet though it was larger, Toronto's early success was still based on the same kind of mercantile econ-omy — the export of agricultural products and timber, and the import of goods required by a rapidly growing British North American colony.

Like Hamilton and Kingston, Toronto had an

James Gooderham built a new mill and distillery in 1859–1861 to replace the original small works, completed in 1832–1837. This print shows the property in 1896 and most of the buildings still stand today as the Distillery District. The Gardiner Expressway and railway tracks now occupy the area of the wharves and open water.

The first locomotive manufactured in Canada was the "Toronto" built in 1853 by the Toronto Locomotive Works for the Ontario Simcoe and Huron Railroad.

excellent, if shallow, harbour. In 1851, water traffic was still the only economical means of moving goods over long distances. Toronto shipping connected with New York City by means of the Erie Canal, which reached Lake Ontario through the port of Oswego. Similarly, the Welland Canal bypassed Niagara Falls to provide a direct link between Lake Ontario and Lake Erie. By the late 1840s, the St. Lawrence River had been made navigable between Lake Ontario and Montreal. The Toronto Harbour Trust, created by the city in 1850 to replace an earlier ineffectual committee, was responsible for dredging the harbour (though it had only negligible control over the privately owned shoreline).

At the same time, while Toronto could export agricultural and forestry products through the ocean ports of Montreal and New York, its inland trading area, or hinterland, at this point was severely limited, due to wretched road conditions. In 1851, the local hinterland extended out from Toronto in an arc of only sixty kilome-

tres (forty miles) — to Durham County to the east, Lake Simcoe to the north and Peel County to the west. During the 1850s all this started to change. A convergence of local, national and international events would propel Toronto very far ahead of its local rivals. Indeed, it began its rise as the dominant city of Canada West, later southern Ontario.

Railways were the agent and symbol of this transformation. The Northern Railway, whose first sod was turned by the governor general's wife, Lady Elgin, in 1851, reached Bradford in 1853 and Collingwood on Georgian Bay in 1855. Farm produce and timber from more northerly forests began to enter the city for onward export by either rail or water. In the 1860s, grain boats from American ports on the upper Great Lakes began rail shipments through Collingwood and expanded Toronto's grain export business. The city's first grain elevator was completed in 1863.

Like Lieutenant-Governor Simcoe's earlier Yonge Street, Toronto's new Northern Railway (known for its first few years as the Ontario, Simcoe & Huron) also followed, in a general sense, the ancient route of the Toronto Passage, from Lake Ontario to Georgian Bay. It would take some considerable time for the strategic logic of this project to reach its full fruition. Yet the Aboriginal canoe-and-portage waterway would live on, as the modern city's pathway to an increasingly expanding northern hinterland, in Ontario and ultimately in Canada at large.

A Great Western Railway locomotive.

THE REGIONAL RAILWAY CITY STARTS TO RISE

In the hope of tapping into Toronto's commerce, Hamilton entrepreneurs in effect built Toronto's second railway, the Great Western, in 1855. The unintended consequence was that their aspirations were reversed: Hamilton was drawn into Toronto's trading orbit, and not the other way around. Still more importantly, the Great Western provided a rail connection to New York State and the burgeoning American market.

The third and final railway to enter Toronto was the Grand Trunk — built by British money and headquartered in Montreal (and sometimes known in Toronto as "the Montreal railway"). For a short time after it was completed in 1859, the Grand Trunk was the world's longest rail line, extending from Portland, Maine, to Detroit, Michigan, through Montreal, Toronto and Sarnia. The company was so convinced that all traffic would move from water to rail that its freight depot in Toronto had no wharfage connections whatsoever. Water traffic remained economically viable, however, and became a complement to railway service. Indeed, after a few years, the Grand Trunk realized its error and acquired its own wharves.

Railway transport was not cheaper than water but it was faster, reaching areas that were not accessible by water. It also operated year-round, not having the limitations of water travel posed by the Canadian winter freeze. During the 1860s, limited funds, the lack of public interest in the harbour and the growing influence of private railway interests led to a marked decline in the maintenance of the harbour.

Railways alone were not sufficient to generate economic growth. The general prosperity of the colony was another significant factor. British industrialization and the Crimean War in Europe had created profitable markets for Canadian wheat overseas, helpful to both farmers and city merchants. In 1854, a Reciprocity Treaty negotiated by the British North American governor general, Lord Elgin, provided for free trade in primary resource products with the United States. (Legend has it that the ebullient and masterful Lord Elgin had thoughtfully also provided

This painting by F.M. Bell-Smith shows the Yonge Street Wharf c.1887 with passengers and their baggage embarking on the paddle steamer Algerian.

The Grand Trunk Railway Station was built in 1873 on the harbour edge near York Street. This facility, with some later additions, remained in use until the present Union Station was finally completed in 1931.

numerous cases of champagne to help get the agreement through the Congress in Washington.) Vigorous, if also intermittently interrupted, new economic growth created enormous increases in export traffic through Toronto.

In addition to dealings in grain and timber, wholesaling — buying from various suppliers and selling a wide range of goods to small hinterland retailers — was a major commercial activity. Wholesalers had access to financing and connections with suppliers that small retailers could never achieve. In the pre-railway era, when the time between an order and delivery represented months, only those with adequate credit survived. Ironically, although railways diminished the transit time, access to good credit would become even more important in the new railway era as businesses grew in size. The wholesale district in Toronto, centred on the rail and shipping facilities at the harbour, continued to do well.

New symbols of modernity began to appear on the back of the new prosperity. Coal gas was first manufactured in 1841, primarily for street lighting. The enterprise would expand in the second half of the nineteenth century. By 1910, when the gas works had reached its maximum size, it covered about two and a half city blocks. Coal gas supplied the city until natural gas became available in the 1950s. Since Toronto's built-up core had expanded beyond the range of easy walking, horse-drawn omnibuses began operating in 1849 on a few major streets. The pinnacle of urban sophistication was achieved in 1861, when the first street railway opened on Yonge Street (incidentally the same year as the first street railway opened in Montreal, which at this point had twice Toronto's population).

In 1867, the rising railway city's regional political status was enhanced when Canada West became the Province of Ontario, in a new Canadian Confederation that would finally stretch from sea to sea. Toronto became the capital of

Built of sandstone, Ontario's impressive new legislative building was completed in 1892.

Meanwhile, the population of Toronto grew in pace with its rise in trade. Most immigrants from outside Canada came from the United Kingdom. Some of the demographic growth was stimulated by the tragedy of the 1847 Irish potato famine. In 1851, the 11,300 Irish-born residents of the city were the single largest cultural group. The predominantly Catholic Irish poor made the Protestant English elite uncomfortable. The international financial collapse of 1857 slowed down transatlantic immigration for a time. But by 1861, the Toronto population had reached 44,800. By 1871, there were some 56,000 people living in the city — virtually all of whom were either Canadian-born or British immigrants, with the exception of 2,000 Americans. The distinctly British North American character of the place, which continued for much of the next hundred years, had already been well established.

COPING WITH URBAN GROWTH

New urban growth created its own problems, and Toronto was inevitably attracted to certain practices of "the parent state" in dealing

Ontario — then and ever since Canada's most populous province. (The new province made do with old Upper Canada's provincial legislative building until an impressive new sandstone structure was completed at Queen's Park in 1892.)

with these problems. Based on a British concept developed in 1823, a Mechanics' Institute had been established in the city as early as 1831, to educate the working classes through the provision of lectures and reading material. By 1883, the

Mechanics' Institute had become outdated, and its assets were transferred to the city government. The following year a municipal public library, the first in Ontario, assumed the old Institute's library service.

Fresh attention was focused on formal education in the 1850s, in the belief that it could create better citizens and reduce poverty and crime. A city-wide public school board organized in 1850 soon led to free education. By 1871, public schooling was compulsory. Toronto also became a centre of progressive

University College, University of Toronto, as painted by Sir Edmund Head in 1858.

colonial higher learning, when the Anglican King's College was transformed into the secular University of Toronto in 1849.

Where education and a diverse range of churches failed to provide a law-abiding character, the local police force, established in 1835, stepped in. This municipal public service was completely reorganized in 1859, when it was removed from the political control of City Council and placed in the hands of a Police Board. Recalcitrant offenders were placed in jail, along with debtors and the mentally ill. Toronto's first substantial facility of this sort, the Home District Jail, had arisen on the former site of the first Parliament of Upper Canada at the foot of Berkeley Street in 1840. The subsequently more famous Don Jail was completed in 1865.

An early need for more organized urban planning also surfaced in the 1850s. The failure of the grand concept of a harbour-side walkway known as the Esplanade showed that something was amiss. In 1818, all of the waterfront land south of Front Street had been privately acquired, but with provision for a continuing public walkway along the lake. Although the concept was clear enough in city plans, little actual improvement was made to the shoreline. The arrival of the Grand Trunk Railway finally forced the construction of the so-called Esplanade, ostensibly as a combination rail corridor and pedestrian promenade. When it was completed in 1858, however, the Esplanade was just a rail corridor filled with tracks. There was no pedestrian promenade and no public access to the city waterfront.

The provision of parks — the "lungs of a city" — was not a pressing issue when Toronto was small. Yet allowances were made for a number

The municipally owned John Street Pumphouse was built in 1877 on a long wharf into the harbour because railways occupied the shoreline.

formed with a conveyance of the estate of the architect John Howard to the city in 1873, although Howard retained use of some of the property until his death in 1890.

The city's urban form began to change as its centre slowly moved from the old town (generally between Yonge and the Don River) to a new focus on Yonge Street. The great fire of 1849 had destroyed four hectares (ten acres) of commercial buildings, and the resultant gaps were filled with several monumental structures of the day. One of the early events held in St. Lawrence Hall on King Street, completed in 1851, was the first "Great North American Convention of Coloured People" — a testament to Canada West's status as a terminus for the Underground Railroad and the strength of abolitionist sentiment in mid-nineteenth-century Toronto. To the south, on Front Street, was the city hall, which had been built in 1845 and survived the 1849 fire. The fire had also led to an ordinance that required all new downtown construction to be of brick.

of attractive public green spaces that still survive. The first public park was a private donation made by the lawyer and politician G.W. Allan between 1857 and 1862. In 1859, the colonial government acquired the land later known as Queen's Park to create another major public space. The city's other large park, High Park, was

The increase in the number of buildings and

The Provincial Lunatic Asylum, as portrayed in watercolour by architect John Howard, 1846.

the growing size of the population called for other infrastructure improvements. Sewers had been among the earliest services of this sort, with trunk lines emptying directly into the harbour. Apart from health and aesthetic issues, this caused headaches for navigation. In the 1850s, there were complaints that sewage was causing the harbour to silt up. By the end of the century, the city owned several dredges to keep docks and slips free of sewage deposits.

The provision of fresh water also became a concern. The same group that had built the coal gas plant had completed a water pumping station in 1841. The waterworks pumped water from the increasingly polluted harbour, primarily for fighting fires within the city. A municipally run waterworks that drew clean water from the lake arrived in 1877. For the first time citizens had a reliable source of drinking water. The facility, now located inside a modern building adjacent to the

Rogers Centre, still remains in use.

Later in the nineteenth century, the city had to accommodate growing numbers of refuse dumps, privies, water supplies and other sanitary dangers. Toronto established a position for a permanent public health officer in 1883. Attitudes towards medicine changed as well. The first General Hospital had been built in 1829, but until the 1870s hospitals typically functioned as places for the poor to get help, and not as centres of good-quality medical treatment. Modern hospitals began to appear with the founding of the Hospital for Sick Children in 1875. By the 1890s, several smaller hospitals had been established. Perhaps reflecting the new stress of the age of progress in the middle of the nineteenth century, Canada West's first provincial asylum was opened in Toronto in 1850.

As early as the 1860s, housing, commerce and industry had almost filled in the official municipal territory established in 1834. To accommodate new growth and obtain a wider tax base, the city embarked on its first wave of annexations in the 1880s. The Village of Yorkville voted for annexation in 1883, to obtain better municipal services. The following year the city expanded eastward across the Don River to acquire the present Riverdale neighbourhood. By 1893, Toronto had annexed a ring of adjacent smaller communities.

THE NEW INDUSTRIAL BASE

Financial collapse following on the heels of prosperity (and vice versa) was a recurring theme in nineteenth-century Toronto, as in other North American cities. Though the Panic of 1857 had brought prosperity to an abrupt end, a new lucrative market supplying Union forces during the American Civil War revived the local economy. Wartime profits ended in 1865, however, and the new US Congress that emerged from the Civil War cancelled the Reciprocity Treaty in 1866. Toronto was slow to feel the impact of another international depression, which began in 1873, and led to another bout of hard times.

In the midst of all this economic turbulence, Toronto began to acquire the increasingly sophisticated manufacturing sector that would do so much to define the local age of industry. In the decades leading up to the railway era, small-scale industrial activity had already played an important role in the growth of the city. Foundries provided ironware for domestic and commercial use, and some became capable of producing complex machinery. For example, in 1853, James Good's Toronto foundry built Canada West's first railway locomotive. The growth of the railways themselves enabled manufacturers to build more efficient and larger factories and to market their products across a wider area. Manufacturers from neighbouring smaller communities were increasingly drawn to Toronto by the new eco-nomic advantages of rail transportation.

The quintessential industrialists were the Massey family. Hart Massey (1823–1896) encouraged his family to relocate their agricultural implement factory from Newcastle, Ontario, to Toronto in 1879. By 1886, the Massey works were Toronto's largest industry. In 1891, the Massey firm combined with the Harris firm from Brantford, Ontario, to create the dominant agricultural implement producer in Canada. In the twentieth century, Massey-Harris would become one of the largest farm machinery producers in the world.

Successful manufacturing — and successful commerce — would also increasingly come to depend on timely information. The local arrival of the telegraph preceded railway construction by almost a decade. In 1847, telegraph wires connected Toronto through Montreal to Quebec City, as well as to the US system at Buffalo, New York. A generation later, in 1879, the city's first telephone exchange was installed, with forty subscribers. The following year it became part of the newly incorporated Bell Telephone Company in Canada. As early as 1850 the city had five newspapers, of which the *Globe*, established in 1844, would become the most influential (as well as the longest-lasting, ancestor of the present-day *Globe and Mail*). Somewhat like today, some newspapers were strongly influenced by political parties. In the nineteenth century, the Liberal Party was identified with the *Globe* and the Conservative Party with the *Mail* (founded in 1872, and later called the *Mail and Empire*). The *Daily Star*, which began in 1892, was at first more independent. The populist *Evening Telegram*, founded in 1876 by John Ross Robertson (1841–1918), brought mass journalism (and its own particular conservative values) to the people of the city.

Toronto Rolling Mills (1864) by William Armstrong. The mills opened in 1857 to re-roll worn out iron rails. When cheaper, stronger steel rails became available, the mill closed, in 1873.

CANADA'S SECOND CITY

In November 1885, the first Canadian Pacific Railway train to cross Canada steamed into the scruffy Pacific port of Port Moody. Vancouver was reached two years later. Much to the chagrin of Toronto's business community, the Canadian Pacific was a Montreal-based company. Because southern Ontario was too large a market for the company to ignore, however, it purchased several local lines radiating out of Toronto, and constructed a main line between the city and Montreal. Toronto's earlier Northern Railway also expanded to North Bay in 1886, in a not altogether happy attempt to link up with the CPR main line through northern Ontario.

Completion of the Canadian Pacific brought several changes to Toronto, which was now Canada's second-largest city, after Montreal. The

CPR drew Western Canada into the city's commercial hinterland. The Massey farm machinery business, for example, opened a warehouse in Winnipeg in 1885. The CPR also ended what had become the Grand Trunk's domination of the Toronto rail traffic of the day. By 1890, most railways in southern Ontario had been amalgamated into either the Canadian Pacific or the Grand Trunk systems (the Northern Railway had itself joined the Grand Trunk in 1888).

The coming of the Canadian Pacific necessitated expansion of the narrow corridor along the harbour that had been set aside for rail access and terminal facilities. Since 1834, the so-called "Windmill Line" (named after the Gooderham and Worts grain-milling windmill) had defined the limit of private ownership on the harbour. With such a clear need for more space south of the Windmill Line, it was thought that landfill in the lake would provide much-needed new terrain for rail improvements and deep-water wharves. Complicated negotiations between the city, railway companies and the federal government dragged on until 1893, when the harbour-filling scheme was finally authorized. Over the next four years the Canadian Pacific built a railway yard on the newly reclaimed land.

Continuing railway development had some impact on local energy use as well. Firewood had been modern Toronto's first major source of energy. While coal was more efficient, transportation costs at first limited its use. Yet by 1876, Gooderham and Worts was importing 8,000 tons of coal annually to produce steam, and coal was the raw material used by the Consumers Gas Company to manufacture gas. During the 1870s, rapidly diminishing forests and improved rail transport to the closest coalfields in Pennsylvania helped make coal prices more affordable. By 1880, virtually all railway locomotives in Ontario had converted from wood to coal. Between 1875 and 1883, coal imports into Toronto more than doubled, from 152,000 to 303,000 tons. Coal imports continued to almost double over every subsequent ten-year period, until the First World War.

Toronto's expanding Canadian hinterland, along with its own population growth, similarly promoted retail sales as an increasingly noteworthy business activity. While King Street had been the prime downtown retail strip, the arrival of Timothy Eaton (1834–1907) from the small Ontario town of St. Marys in 1869, and Robert Simpson (1834–1897) from nearby Newmarket in 1872, altered shopping habits in the city. Eaton's and Simpson's, at Queen and Yonge somewhat north of the earlier King Street strip, perfected local variations on the concept of the department store, which was also starting to appear in other North American cities.

The establishment of mail-order shopping by Eaton's in 1884, and shortly thereafter by Simpson's, was a further innovation. Now anyone in Ontario could enjoy the same products as those available in Toronto. By the early twentieth century, Eaton's was delivering catalogues to the tents of new settlers on the endless prairie of Western Canada. Smaller storeowners found these retail trends as disturbing as their successors would find "big-box" retailing in the 1990s. Retailing generally had become a larger business than wholesaling by the turn of the century, since large retailers increasingly bought directly from suppliers rather than through wholesalers. But this was a relative trend. In absolute numbers, wholesaling continued to grow.

Toronto's expanding hinterland helped stimulate a growing range of banking, insurance and other financial services. The Canadian Bank of Commerce had been founded in 1867 (the same year as Canadian Confederation) to repair the wreckage caused by the 1866 failure of the city's earlier Bank of Upper Canada. Within a few years, the Commerce was by far the largest of several Toronto banks. For a few more generations

Montreal would remain the financial capital of Canada (and "Canada's first bank" — the Bank of Montreal — would remain considerably larger than any Toronto bank). But Toronto took some fresh strides in this direction during the late nineteenth and early twentieth centuries, partly as a result of changes induced by the Montreal-headquartered Canadian Pacific Railway.

New railway development into northern Ontario also helped open up new mining industries in the same region, and this would further strengthen the Toronto financial community. The original Toronto Stock Exchange had been established in 1852, but it did not move into permanent office quarters until 1881. In 1899, a second stock exchange, the Toronto Stock and Mining Exchange, was organized to trade speculative mining equities. This exchange was succeeded by the Standard Stock and Mining Exchange in 1908, which, in turn, merged in 1934 with the original Toronto Stock Exchange, and moved into new quarters on Bay Street.

Maggie, the first Eaton's delivery horse, at the first store at Queen and Yonge, Toronto, around 1869.

THE EARLY TWENTIETH-CENTURY BOOM

As the nineteenth century progressed, Toronto's hinterland became an important source of new urban residents — as important as overseas immigration. Large numbers of people moved from rural Ontario to urban centres. Southern Ontario's profitable farmland was now completely occupied, and increasing farm mechanization (manufactured by companies such as Massey) was reducing the need for rural labourers. Many sons and daughters of farm families were compelled to look to Toronto for employment.

By the start of the twentieth century, things

Toronto's business district, almost 20 acres of buildings along Bay Street, from Wellington south to the railway tracks at the Esplanade, was destroyed by fire overnight April 19, 1904. These images north from Front Street along Bay show before and after. The buildings were quickly rebuilt and the city installed a modern high-pressure fire-hydrant system.

had changed again, and a new boom was in progress. The twenty years preceding the First World War marked a long era of fresh economic prosperity for Toronto, for Ontario and the rest of Canada. Along with forestry and mining in northern Ontario, the settlement of the Western Canadian prairies and the flood of grain coming east for export seemed to offer endless possibilities. Into this market entered the Canadian Northern Railway, the final national railway to reach Toronto. Unlike the two "Montreal railways," the Canadian Pacific and the Grand Trunk, the Canadian Northern was "Toronto's railway." Its head office was located at the east end of the banking district on King Street. Its most prominent owner was William Mackenzie (1849–1923), who also acquired control of the Toronto street railway system. The company started by constructing prairie branch lines in the 1890s, but within ten years it had embarked on building a transcontinental railway to compete with the Canadian Pacific and Grand Trunk.

Lake shipping was expected to help carry the cornucopia of western grain to various ocean ports. The Welland Canal was enlarged. The Toronto Harbour's last major improvement had been dredging the entrance channel in the 1880s. Now it seemed that the waterfront, after decades of neglect by tight-fisted businessmen running the Harbour Trust, was in for a renaissance. The first step, taken in 1911, was to replace the Trust with an independent Toronto Harbour Commission. The following year the new Harbour Commission presented a comprehensive plan for the redevelopment of the harbour to accommodate industry, shipping and recreation. A principal component of the plan included extensive landfilling in the harbour to create new industrial land. Work started on the plan but was interrupted by the First World War.

The new boom lifted the Toronto manufacturing sector as well. Manufacturing in Canada had already received a boost in 1879, when the federal

Artist's portrayal of Toronto Harbour, circa 1927.

government in Ottawa introduced a high tariff on imports of manufactured goods. This tariff was part of a new "National Policy" of Canadian economic development. In theory, this had the effect of removing cheaper American products from domestic markets, enabling Canadian manufacturers to operate profitably (in a country with a vast rugged geography and few people). Enterprising US companies avoided paying import duties on their goods by establishing manufacturing branch plants — and new industrial jobs — in Canada. Canadian General Electric became one of the most successful branch plants established in Toronto. The predecessor company began as a Canadian franchise operation of an American firm. Later it became the Canadian subsidiary of the General Electric Company. Unlike many other branch plants, it then became a wholly owned Canadian company from 1893 until 1923, after which it was again the subsidiary of its US parent firm.

Development extended along the Toronto waterfront, which remained heavily industrialized into the 1950s. Away from the harbour, construction of Canadian Pacific Railway shops at West Toronto in the 1880s acted as a stimulus for the northerly extension of industrial districts; for example, the opening of the Heintzman Piano factory in 1888. By 1901, with the new economic boom in motion, the Junction — a popular name for West Toronto because of its rail connections — supported nine factories employing some 1,200 people. Another local enterprise was the Union Stock Yards, which opened around the turn of the century to replace the overcrowded yards at Toronto Harbour. By the early twentieth century, meat-packing was an important industry in the city. The local William Davies & Co. was "the largest pork-packing firm in the British Empire," and Toronto was sometimes referred to as "Hogtown."

As Massey and Harris demonstrated, the new economic boom could lead to mergers among older manufacturing companies, as well as the creation of new enterprises. Similar trends were at work in the financial sector. The first decade of the twentieth century saw a major consolidation of Toronto-based banks, increasing the already prominent position of the Bank of Commerce (which rapidly became a national bank, with branches from coast to coast in Canada).

COPING WITH MORE URBAN GROWTH

Not all of Toronto's population shared the good life equally. While some industrialists became wealthy, as elsewhere in nineteenth- and early-twentieth-century North America, many factory workers were poorly paid, and their workplace conditions were largely unregulated. Formation of labour organizations seemed to be the only way to present a strong, common negotiating front against owners. Toronto was not particularly notable for significant improvements in labour conditions, although numerous efforts were made over the years. Printers at the *Globe* newspaper, for example, had gone out on one of the earliest strikes in 1854. Even in the new economic boom of the early twentieth century, rising costs with flat wages were hard on workers. Local union membership rose quite dramatically before the First World War, and there was a new burst of industrial unrest (and even political radicalism) after the war ended. But real and lasting progress would elude the labour movement until the late 1930s and the Second World War.

New immigration and a second wave of annexation nonetheless prompted strong population growth. The geographic area of the official City of Toronto doubled between 1891 and 1912 — from 44 to 88 square kilometres (17 to 34 square miles). The population grew from 181,000 in 1891 to 378,000 in 1911. The further additions of North Toronto and Moore Park in 1912 were the last major municipal annexations in the old city until 1967. Throughout the 1920s, the city opposed annexation, partly from a con-

cern that it would benefit only large land developers. These speculators would profit from the extension of costly urban services into undeveloped land. Instead, assorted new suburban municipalities were incorporated in old rural townships, with such names as Swansea, Leaside and East York.

Just before the building boom that accompanied the new economic boom ended, local government efforts were undertaken to control indiscriminate subdivision of land. This started a trend away from the nineteenth-century *laissez-faire* attitudes to urban growth. Land use planning began in 1904 when the city obtained provincial authority to specify the location for stores, industries and other activities that might affect the functioning of the city. While legislation was regulating residential growth, new technology was changing the shape of buildings in the downtown core. The advent of electricity for elevators and lighting, combined with inexpensive steel framing, led to the first high-rise buildings. In 1895, the ten-storey Temple Building on Bay Street became Toronto's first modest skyscraper. Several more were erected prior to the First World War, including the fifteen-storey Canadian Pacific Railway building (1913) and the twenty-storey Royal Bank building (1915).

By the turn of the century, the city was acquiring many trappings of the high-culture global civilization of the British Empire, modified by a rising Canadian nationalism. The Art Gallery of Ontario was established in 1900 and the Royal Ontario Museum in 1912. Business leaders played a critical role in both these projects, under the leadership of Edmund Walker (1848–1924), president of the Bank of Commerce. Hart Massey, a great supporter of music, gave the new Massey Music Hall to the city in 1894. Lawren Harris (1885–1970), the grandson of Hart Massey's farm-machinery business partner, would become one of the locally

The Toronto Suburban Railway on Davenport Road, just west of Bathurst, 1923. This company operated an electric, inter-urban railway service from Toronto to Guelph. Between 1900 and 1920, other inter-urban railways radiated out from Toronto to Scarborough, Lake Simcoe, and Port Credit.

famous "Group of Seven" artists, who specialized in Canadian wilderness landscapes. Modern Toronto had also aged sufficiently to reflect upon its past. John Ross Robertson, owner of the *Evening Telegram*, published *Landmarks of Toronto* in several volumes between 1894 and 1914 based on articles on Toronto's past that had appeared in his newspaper.

THE OLD NEIGHBOURHOOD LIFE

The decline and resurrection of Fort York reflect-

ed other changes in the city of the late nineteenth and early twentieth centuries. The British military had withdrawn from Canada in 1870, just after the 1867 Confederation. A fledgling Canadian army acquired Toronto's two forts. The city acquired the properties in 1903 and promptly decided to demolish part of old Fort York for a new streetcar line. The proposal was rejected by a municipal plebiscite in 1909 — urban growth at all costs was no longer acceptable. The fort was restored and opened as a historic site in 1934.

The proper observance of religious restrictions

A house in "The Ward," winter, 1912. Much of the Ward — an area bounded by University Avenue, College, Yonge and Queen Streets — contained slum housing and was where many new immigrants first settled.

on Sundays remained an arena for civic discourse well into the twentieth century. In one confrontational situation, interests of the street railway company advocating Sunday service and labourers' desires for easy access to parks and recreation sites on their day off were pitted against clergymen and devout business leaders. In 1897, a city plebiscite narrowly approved Sunday streetcar service. Conversely, the religious lobby was able to close municipal toboggan slides in city parks on winter Sundays. The proper purpose of Sunday continued to be debated; it was only a thin majority of Torontonians who voted in 1950 to allow Sunday sports.

The church was also allied with the temperance movement in early-twentieth-century North America. The Town of West Toronto officially took up the temperance position in 1904 when it voted itself dry under "local option" legislation. Five years later the town was annexed by Toronto. During prohibition in Ontario, which more or less effectively lasted from 1916 to 1927, the former town was in step with the rest of the province. Re-establishment of public drinking facilities in Toronto came back slowly, and was not fully realized until 1947. Even then the last holdout district of West Toronto would remain dry by local option until 1998, since the area had retained the right to make its own choice in the 1909 annexation agreement.

During the nineteenth century, people either rented houses or boarded in others' houses, as high housing costs induced by the new economic boom of the early twentieth century prevented many from owning their own homes. In 1921, the city estimated that less than half its householders owned the places where they lived. Although the concept of apartments as a form of affordable housing was becoming popular elsewhere, a 1912 city by-law prevented apartment construction. In 1921, the city contained only 2,200 apartment units out of a total of 98,600 housing units. But the demand for inexpensive housing, especially after the First World War, resulted in circumvention of the by-law. Within ten years, apartments accounted for about seventeen percent of the Toronto housing stock.

The comfortable uniformity of the British ethnicity that the nineteenth century had established in Toronto — comfortable as long as you were of British origin — was first seriously challenged by a substantial, if still far from overwhelming, wave of wider European (and even a little other) immigration, in the fifteen years preceding the First World War. In 1901, 92 percent of the city's population was of British origin, but within ten years that statistic had fallen to 86 percent. The single largest group of new arrivals were East European Jews. By 1931, Jewish people (including Toronto's earlier and more affluent "Old Community" Jews, many of whom had originally come from the United Kingdom) made up 7 percent of the population.

Because new immigrants were also frequently poor and drawn to impoverished areas, their presence drew attention to the city's urban poverty. The so-called Ward, west of Bay Street and between Dundas and College streets, was the most visible such area in the city, because it was so close to the central business district, and even

across the street from City Hall. Other pockets of poverty were scattered around the city, such as Regent Park in Cabbagetown, and what later became known as St. James Town east of Parliament Street. Various municipal commissions were established between 1907 and 1918 to attack the lack of affordable housing. The dominant political belief of the day, however, was that the marketplace could solve this problem. In the end, the city's municipal government would build only about two hundred houses by 1930. Not until after the Second World War did Toronto seriously confront its problems of poverty. The replacement of substandard housing in Regent Park did not start until 1947.

NEW URBAN INFRASTRUCTURE

Just as coal had fuelled nineteenth-century industrial growth, electricity became essential in the twentieth century — not just in industry, but also for office and domestic use. The city's first commercial generating station started to produce electricity for street lighting in 1882. By 1900, all electrical utilities had been consolidated into the Toronto Electric Light Company. The Toronto Street Railway — or, more formally, the Toronto Railway Company — was its largest customer, and in fact, it was the largest consumer of power in Ontario. Initially, electricity was produced in the city with steam-powered generating stations. With an ever-increasing demand for electric power in Toronto, the owners of the street railway obtained waterpower rights at Niagara Falls in 1903, and Toronto started to receive Niagara power in 1906.

For a time the Toronto Electric Light Company had a monopoly over the supply of electric power in the city. The high cost and poor service made the company increasingly unpopular as electricity became more essential to economic growth and quality of life. After a

A flying boat in front of the Toronto Harbour Commissioners building, May 1921. The Commissioners established a full "air harbour" for floatplanes in 1929. In 1937, the city built two land-based airports, one on Toronto Island, the other at Malton, now Pearson International Airport. Today the Harbour Commissioners building is well inland from the waterfront.

decade of debate, the City of Toronto allied with other Ontario municipalities in urging the provincial government to create the publicly owned Hydro-Electric Power Commission of Ontario in 1906 to generate and distribute electric power. The city set up the Toronto Hydro Commission to provide local distribution. The Toronto Electric Light Company continued to compete with the municipal system until 1922, when the Toronto system was purchased by the city and Ontario Hydro acquired the Niagara generating station.

In the early twentieth century, Toronto's street railway was privately operated under a franchise from the city government. In 1891, the city briefly owned the system, but voters objected to the cost of its upgrading and it was re-tendered

for private operation. The new thirty-year franchise required the owners to modernize operations, replacing earlier horse-hauled streetcars with self-propelled electric cars over a two-year period. Despite these improvements, the city and its citizens were soon in conflict with the company over the quality of its service. An insufficient number of cars produced crowded, infrequent transportation. By 1912, annexation had doubled the city's area and twenty percent of its population now lay beyond the existing streetcar rail network. The company steadfastly ignored municipal pressure to expand its lines beyond its franchise territory of 1891. In 1910–1911, the city decided to construct three essential routes into annexed areas and operate

Toronto Island in 1896, *Harry Spiers. The island was created by a storm in 1858 that resulted in a channel across the east end of the peninsula. In the 1870s, the City of Toronto started to rent lots on the island and built a boardwalk. Ferry companies provided connections to the mainland.*

them separately as the Toronto Civic Railway.

The habits of the privately operated Toronto Street Railway became so unpopular that there was no question that the service would become a municipal responsibility when the franchise expired. The Toronto Transportation (today Transit) Commission (TTC) was incorporated to acquire all street railways, once the private franchise expired in September 1921. The city immediately started a program to rebuild most of the track, acquire new rolling stock and generally modernize the service. It also started to run buses to coordinate with the streetcars. Soon the city had a modern, robust transit infrastructure. The TTC was able to survive an investment drought during the 1930s Depression and the Second World War, and still remain in generally good condition.

Continual improvements were also required in the local public waterworks, to ensure both quality and quantity. A major expansion of the city-wide service came with the completion in 1935 of a new waterworks, ultimately known as the R.C. Harris pumping station. It was notable not only as a large modern piece of civil engineering, but also as a striking example of public-works architecture. More sewers were built as well. The city's first sanitary sewage treatment plant was opened in 1913, on the shore of Ashbridge's Bay. Solid waste was becoming a matter of municipal concern too. Throughout the nineteenth century, the city had used the harbour as a dumping ground for garbage. Since most waste was coal ash from furnaces and stoves, the material made convenient landfill. As dumping grounds on the waterfront disappeared and the volume and character of waste changed, Toronto built its first garbage incinerators in 1893 and 1896.

Prince Edward viaduct under construction, 1916. It was completed in 1918 and removed the impediment of the deep Don River Valley to eastward urban growth.

BETWEEN THE WARS

Canada's rapid economic growth ended the year before the start of the First World War (1914–1918). By 1916, military demands had revived industrial production, and Toronto benefited greatly. But in other ways the war brought great local tragedy. The city sent seventy thousand of its youngest citizens to the Canadian forces fighting in Europe, but one in seven did not return.

Once the fighting ended, earlier projects interrupted by the war started up again. The opening of Sunnyside Amusement Park on the west-end waterfront, in the spring of 1922, was the most public manifestation of the Harbour Commission's postwar resumption of work on its 1912 development plan. Expansion of the

harbour lands elsewhere along the waterfront was completed in 1930.

While the Harbour Commission was extending the harbour lands, the Canadian Pacific and the Grand Trunk railways were remodelling their waterfront facilities. The Grand Trunk's station had been a union station since the 1850s — not at the preference of the companies involved, but because of a lack of space for separate terminals. Travellers benefited from the convenience of this single station, but the railways would have preferred their own facilities, in their competition with one another for business. Despite a number of expansions to the Grand Trunk's building, the station remained a cobbled-together affair. Construction of a union station that was truly appropriate for Toronto's status as Canada's second city did not

Sunnyside Park on Victoria Day, 1929. When Sunnyside opened in 1922, its easy accessibility to the city marked the end of the amusement monopoly provided by Hanlan's Point Park on Toronto Island.

start until 1914. Delays brought about by the First World War and changes in the design of the station delayed its completion. The new Union Station on Front Street was not fully operational until 1931. By then the Grand Trunk had become part of a new Canadian National Railways system, owned by the federal government in Ottawa.

Another great change along the waterfront was the grade separation of railway tracks and city roads. By the start of the twentieth century, the track barrier to pedestrian and road traffic was formidable. In 1912, a traveller down John Street had to cross twenty-five different railway tracks. Planning for the separation of road and rail traffic had begun in 1882. By the time designs for the new Union Station were being developed, both the city and the railways realized that grade separation was an essential component of the project, though the precise means of achieving this were not finalized until 1924. The road and pedestrian underpasses that were eventually built to cross the railway lands still serve the city today.

Canadians were cautiously optimistic about their economy during the earlier and middle parts of the roaring 1920s. Then the three years

Snowbound Downtown, *1938, by Nicholas Hornyansky. The Bank of Commerce building is in the centre and the Royal York Hotel is to the right.*

following 1926 saw a dramatic economic boom that ultimately proved too speculative. In this climate, the earlier changes to Toronto's downtown skyline that had been interrupted by the First World War were resumed. Fourteen skyscrapers were built between 1922 and 1928. A new Bank of Commerce head office on King Street, not completed until 1931, was thirty-four storeys high — and qualified as the "tallest building in the British Empire." The new Royal York Hotel, which opened in 1929, was similarly hailed as "the largest hotel in the British Empire." In fact, New York City's Empire State Building, also completed in 1931, had 102 storeys, but this did little to dampen local enthusiasm for Toronto's own new skyscrapers. Then the optimism and financial daring that had helped make all this possible came to a spectacular end, with the international stock-market crash in October of 1929.

Meanwhile, at some point in the 1920s, the automobile in Canada had moved well beyond being a toy for the rich. By 1931, Ontario had the highest registration of vehicles per capita in Canada, and Toronto had the highest in Ontario. Car ownership in the city increased from some 10,000 in 1916 to 80,000 in 1928.

The city's nineteenth-century street grid had been laid out for slow-moving pedestrian and horse-drawn traffic. Automobiles and trucks created new challenges for urban traffic flow. A major problem in the core area could be traced back to the original survey for the city. Large "park lots" for aspiring landed gentry had originally been laid out between Queen and Bloor streets. By the 1860s, these estates were being subdivided and new east-west roads constructed across each lot. The roads from one subdivision seldom met directly with those of adjacent lots. The resulting jogs restricted automobile traffic, and created a need for connecting links that would improve the flow of east-west traffic.

Since the major north-south streets had been the boundaries of the "park lots," these roads ran straight to the harbour and did not require any realignment for motor vehicle traffic. As early as 1926, the city established a Joint Traffic Committee to review the ability of city streets to carry motor vehicle traffic, but little was done at the time. Another traffic plan produced in 1930 advocated widening the north-south streets, because of heavy traffic, and building the much-needed east-west connector links. With the arrival of the 1930s Depression, however only limited road improvements of any sort were actually undertaken. But in the city's wider hinterland the new Queen Elizabeth Way would be opened in 1939. It started at the Humber River, and ultimately linked Toronto to New York State at Buffalo. It was one of the earliest four-lane, controlled-access highways in North America. A 1943 City of Toronto transportation plan would call for an extensive series of urban superhighways to be built after the Second World War. Fortunately, few of these freeways came to be, but the plans for their construction foreshadowed the new degree of automobile dominance that lay ahead.

THE GREAT DEPRESSION (AND WAR AGAIN)

If managing automobile traffic was a bane for early as well as later city planners, the growing popularity of motor vehicles certainly helped Toronto's own industrial growth. Although the city did not have any large assembly plants within its own borders, many of its factories produced automotive components. In 1925, some five per-

cent of industrial employment was in motor vehicle industries, broadly defined. Goodyear Tire, for example, had opened a Toronto branch plant before the First World War. By 1920, it was producing several thousand tires a day.

The 1930s Depression hit Toronto as hard as most other cities — though gold and silver mining in northern Ontario helped keep some parts of the Bay Street financial sector in above-average economic health. Except for a few projects begun in the prosperous 1920s, new building construction came to a virtual standstill. Immigration slowed as well, only reviving again after the Second World War. Then there was a massive increase in unemployment. In 1933, as much as thirty percent of the city's population was out of work. Relief agencies were formed to help ease at least some of the hardships that many city residents had to endure. The city and the adjacent suburban municipalities tried to employ more people in such public works projects as laying water mains and building sewers. Though the worst of the Depression was over by 1935, lingering high unemployment would only be ended altogether by the Second World War.

The City of Toronto had no interest in annexation during the 1930s. The neighbouring new suburban municipalities were actually in greater financial difficulty, and formed a kind of ring of trouble around the city. In 1931, some 187,000 people lived in these ring suburbs, compared with about 631,000 in the city. Disparities in levels of public transit service was only one of the major hurdles that the suburban communities faced. The TTC provided good service within the official city boundaries, but only minimal bus service extended into the suburbs. Disparities of this sort would not be completely eliminated until the 1970s.

The Second World War, from the summer of 1939 to the spring and summer of 1945, finally brought back full employment. Canada was in

Unemployed workers sleeping in the bandstand at Queen's Park, Toronto, 1938

the war from start to finish. Much wartime industrial production was focused in central Canada, and brought large benefits to Toronto. War industries pumped money into the city. Although the outcome of the war was the most immediate concern, municipal planning for readjustment to a civilian economy started early. In 1943, the city created the Toronto Reconstruction Council, hoping the war would end in victory relatively soon. A comprehensive municipal plan was released in 1943, providing a vision of development over the course of the next thirty years.

In hindsight, the end of the war in 1945 formed a symbolic point of transition from the previous century of urban growth driven by industrialization to the modern economically diverse metropolitan city of today. Gooderham and Worts continued distilling spirits on the same property it had first started to develop a century earlier. Fort York, on the other hand, no longer served to protect national interests; it had been transformed into a historic site and tourist attraction. The city possessed a relatively solid infrastructure of public transit, water and hydro — and a rather high-quality local public education system. Much of the population was still very British North American in its origins and traditions. Lurking beyond the city's official borders were growing suburbs that hid the true scale of Toronto's future and would prove to be the foundations for some phenomenal new postwar growth and transition.

Chapter 5

TORONTO INTO THE TWENTY-FIRST CENTURY

Roger Hall

TORONTO AND THE SECOND WORLD WAR

Torontonians by their thousands poured joyously into the streets on VE day in May 1945 and celebrated VJ day just as enthusiastically three months later. A stranger observing these unfettered demonstrations might have been forgiven for thinking that Toronto was a completely changed city from the introverted capital that had entered the war in 1939. In many ways, however, the change was merely a gloss. Toronto at war's end was still staid, sanctimonious, basically British, Protestant and shut up on Sundays. Nevertheless, below the bland

"Toronto's City Hall became the focal point for teeming thousands," reported the Globe and Mail *of VE day celebrations on May 7, 1945. "Servicemen and their girlfriends hopped onto running boards, perched on car bumpers and even straddled the hoods of the vehicles. Nobody cared." The paper called it a "Carnival of Joy." "In many a church and in the privacy of homes, were those who prayed and wept. For these the victory was bought at great price."*

Top: More than 400 Lancaster heavy bombers were turned out at the Victory Aircraft Company's Malton factory. In this photo, workers are shown surrounding and adorning the hundredth plane — produced in 1944 but, sadly, shot down in Germany the following year.

Left: Initials were everywhere — there was D-Day, VE Day and VJ Day, but N-Day meant the war was really over. It was February 19, 1946 — and the N stood for Nylons, basically unseen since the war's earliest days since the synthetic was a restricted item needed for parachutes. Some 3,000 people were reported to have joined snaking lines outside Toronto stores to get a pair — or two or three.

surface a progressive mood stirred, one that had been set in motion during the six years of conflict and would eventually shake earnest, sedate Toronto to its sober roots.

War is sometimes called the locomotive of history — an event that pushes and pulls economies and societies into fresh territories at a vigorous and aggressive pace. And so it was for Toronto. During the six years of war, the lakeside city became an industrial nexus for the Allied war effort. New factories sprang up in suburbs and adjacent communities — perhaps the most celebrated being the Victory plant at Malton, where ten thousand toiled to produce four-engined Lancaster bombers. Within the old city, domestic manufacturers, like Inglis and Massey–Harris, shifted from home appliances and agricultural equipment to war *matériel* — turning out everything from munitions to machine guns and other weapons. Elsewhere, in places as unlikely as the stables at Casa Loma, skilled workers designed and developed high-tech optical and electronic equipment for use in submarine detection.

A huge shipyard sprawled where Spadina Avenue met the lake, and by 1945 it had turned out fifty minesweepers for Canadian and British forces.

Total war meant total commitment for the city in social and cultural terms as well. Uniforms were the order of the day, from standard military to industrial coveralls to utilitarian civvy fashions. Temporary barracks, as in the First World War, were erected on open lands throughout the city; recruits and returned soldiers seemed everywhere, not least in the vicinity of the many military hospitals large and small. All of these thousands of war workers had to be housed, and housing was in short supply, so a trend that had begun in the Depression continued: grand Victorian and Edwardian houses were split into small apartments or made over into rooming houses "just for the duration."

Without doubt, the best-known wartime housing community was "Little Norway" at the foot of Bathurst Street, adjacent to the Toronto Island Airport. Here, Norwegian flyers and service personnel lived, trained and worked from 1940 to 1943. But the hastily thrown-up barracks lasted much longer — "for the duration" in this case meant emergency housing, and the emergency went on for some time; the huts were finally torn down in 1958.

While the war heated up and redirected the economy, the dominant society and the cloying culture of the old provincial town persisted. Wyndham Lewis, the English writer, was there during the war and called TO "a sanctimonious ice-box . . . this bush-metropolis of the Orange Lodges." It certainly looked that way: civic spirit was something that happened elsewhere. In fact, spirits (of all sorts) largely happened elsewhere or behind closed residential doors. It was simply impossible to get a drink without a meal (and restaurant meals were mediocre at best). On the other hand, *formal* spirituality, particularly of the Protestant variety, was clearly triumphant, with church on Sunday (and lit-

A military wedding at Stanley Barracks within the CNE grounds: this photograph dates to the beginning of hostilities in 1939 because the men wear uniforms of both First and Second World War design. By the end of the year, a volunteer battalion from the 48th Highlanders portrayed here had been sent to England.

tle else) virtually compulsory behaviour. At least the streetcars ran (doubtless to get the faithful to worship), but organized sport had no niche, and movies and concerts were frowned upon. As for public art, beyond solemn statuary and the odd handsome building, it was unknown, with even exuberant graffiti unborn at the time. And when Victory finally came, there wasn't a dignified, central place to celebrate, except the tiny footprint that served the purpose in front of the City Hall. Toronto was, as the great literary critic and long-time citizen Northrop Frye would later declare, a good place to mind your own business.

A FRESH DYNAMIC

One legacy of the wartime years proved indelible and eventually transformed provincial Toronto into both metropolis and cosmopolis: big government — big, invasive, intrusive and sometimes impudent government. A country at war had been used to the idea of authority — at that juncture the power was more federal, but edicts and regulations filtered down, with not a few issuing from provincial and municipal sources. Moreover, many considered big government the most efficient and progressive way to provide a share of the prosperity for all. That opportunity had been glimpsed provincially with the strong popular showing of the socialist Co-operative Commonwealth Federation (the CCF, the forerunner of today's New Democratic Party) in the provincial election of 1943, but it was there too in George Drew's famous and durable Tory "twenty-two points" platform, which ensured the Progressive Conservatives would become, in many minds, the "government party."

The basis of this ongoing Tory success was "brokerage politics," a negotiation process between voters and politicians where the public was carefully consulted — polled and cajoled — in the building of any Tory proposal, with the result that, in legislative terms, the voters appeared to get what they wanted. Provincial government, reflecting wartime experience, thought and acted comprehensively and managerially. Central planning — a phrase that today has something of a Soviet ring — had won the war and might now secure the peace for everyone. Society would not be levelled, but the economic pie could be made larger, so that everyone might get a piece. Moreover, stability at the provincial level provided huge potential opportunities for growth at other governmental levels, not least municipal ones. As a result, Ontario's Tories, under such leaders as Colonel George Drew, Leslie Frost, John Robarts and William Davis, created, beginning in the war, a dynasty at Queen's Park that lasted more than four decades.

Planning for a better postwar Toronto had its start during those war years. As early as 1943, as noted, a Toronto Reconstruction Council was created to avoid the social and economic challenges that were evident at the end of the First World War. A year later, in 1944, the province established a Department of Planning and Development, followed two years later by a provincial Planning Act. Although urban planning was not compulsory for municipalities, it was greatly encouraged by this action.

Prosperity would help — but it needed coaxing to come fully on stream. Federal initiatives like unemployment insurance helped individuals survive job changes, and the family-allowance programs, introduced in 1946, helped feed and clothe children; the development of the Rand Formula that same year ensured that all workers in a particular job area might profit from labour settlements. But general well-being at war's end remained too much "around the corner" for most Canadians faced with shortages of consumer goods and a severe housing crisis. Torontonians, more practical than ideological, looked to the left-wing to provide needed benefits, and in municipal and provincial contests threw voter support behind the CCF, with some going further, even electing Communists like Joe Salsberg (who was both an alderman and an MPP).

Despite all this wartime and postwar activity, however, the city's population had not grown — in fact, the central city shrank. The old Ontario amalgam of small towns and their hinterlands still held an attraction for itinerant wartime workers, and many at war's end returned to their rural and small-town roots. In 1945 the old city of Toronto's population stood at 681,802. Five years later it had declined to 667,487, not a huge drop but significant. What had grown were the outlying suburbs and towns. North York jumped in those five years from 26,432 to 62,646, Etobicoke doubled in size to 44,000, and Scarborough did the same, reaching almost 50,000. Regardless of this growth, the Toronto region's social complexion had not been notably altered, as so much of the influx had been from the traditional British sources, a measurable percentage being war brides.

A fully charged and dynamic economy would modify this dramatically. That confluence of energies — of capital, labour and expanding markets — occurred at about the mid-century mark. Again war was one of the drivers, this time in Korea, a conflict that helped re-kindle industrial initiatives and guaranteed well-paid jobs. As well, the housing market boomed, not least

Toronto still hasn't abandoned its beloved streetcars but many lines have been ripped up, not least in the city core and in the wake of subway alternatives. Here we see the last run of the Bay-Dupont line. The car is one of the famous Peter Witt designs that first went into service in the 1920s.

because of monies made more easily available through government plans — notably the Central Mortgage and Housing Corporation (CMHC), established in 1946 to help veterans and then extended to Canadians generally. Improved and increased housing growth was crucial for any number of reasons, as the building stock had dwindled during the long Depression and wartime years. But the explanation for so much of the buoyancy and largesse was simpler, indeed rudimentary: the baby

boom, officially charted back to 1947 but with a noteworthy bounce by 1945. All these new mouths meant expansion at every level — agriculture, schools, transportation. As well, after 1950, the country's doors were thrown open to immigrants from former enemy countries, and Germans and Italians, keen to escape the gloom of bombed-out Europe, eagerly joined displaced persons, economic migrants and refugees who flocked to peaceful North America and particularly

Torontonians came from everywhere — and they are still coming. Clockwise from left, an Italian family of the 1950s, two Ojibway women, a mix of Guyanese and Greek newcomers and a recent Somali cultural event — from one of the most multicultural cities anywhere.

to its large urban centres. At long last as well, Chinese exclusionary acts were tossed out and a trickle of Asian immigration (which would eventually turn into a torrent) began.

Sombre old Toronto did not exactly welcome this huge influx with open arms ("DP" for "displaced person" was almost a racial slur), but neither was there huge hostility. The upper echelons of society did not change. It was still the "Masseys and the Masses," even if the masses did not all originate in the old sod. Significantly, these new immigrants were willing — indeed enthusiastic — to take on the hard physical labour of servicing the booming economy. Rare was a construction site where Italian was not the language of work; rarer the factory floor that did not ring to the mixed cadences of a dozen different European tongues. The crucible of a cosmopolis was being created — and with amazing speed.

Toronto, of course, was not the only centre of this unparalleled expansion. But it led the way — and in so doing confirmed the gradual eclipse of its old rival, Montreal. Toronto was the provincial capital that sported convenient links between government and business. Besides, Toronto's connections to the United States, firmly established in war, blossomed in peace (physical proximity to American markets didn't hurt either). Also instrumental was the coming of the St. Lawrence Seaway, which permitted seaborne traffic into the centre of the continent, and the fact that Montreal's manufacturing infrastructure was antiquated. Toronto was English-speaking, English being the principal language of the continent, and this was no small attraction to immigrants eager for a slice of the American dream or to Western Canadians looking for better jobs.

Typical of the post-war period was the subdivision Kipling Heights, which sprawled north of the 401. In this photograph from the 1960s, one can still see touches of the virgin countryside to the north.

Moreover, Toronto, unrestricted geographically compared with Montreal's insularity, had plenty of space in which to grow.

Suburbia was not invented in the 1950s — Toronto had had streetcar suburbs such as the Annex, where people lived separately from their work for many decades, and the old Belt Line railway, looping up the Don Valley and then stretching westward through the northern extents of the city, was the very definition of a suburban link bringing commuters into town. And Toronto had frequently expanded territorially, usually by reaching out and consuming existing villages in its hinterland — places such as Yorkville which already had the nuclei of human activity: shops, churches, local services and markets, and sometimes local governments. But the 'burbs that flowered in the fifties were different.

It took the unique intersection of a strengthening economy, the continuing housing shortage, the baby boom, the influx of immigrants and responsive (some would later call it irresponsible) government to create suburbia. Added to this was the persuasive idea that centralized cities (as had characterized Europe so recently) were, if not evil, capable of harbouring evil, and so there was a yearning for open spaces, wide green lawns and the fresh unfetid air of the countryside. The inner city might be a place to earn your crust, but your real life — the life of family, health and repose — required a quieter, more contemplative and protected place, a place where a growing family might possess community and privacy at the same time: a place of freedom. And what would make all that possible? Better pay and reasonable borrowing rates with which to build the nest, to be sure, but most significantly, private ownership of the automobile.

Emblematic of these new suburbs for Toronto was Don Mills, where construction began in 1952. At first planners had thought the place might be a "new town" on the British model of Letchworth or Welwyn Garden City. But the site up the Don Valley was just too close to downtown, so before long Don Mills became the archetypal suburban bedroom community, with a segregated shopping and business centre, a community centre, reserved areas for churches and schools, and tracts and tracts of new, mostly similar and mostly affordable housing. Every part of it was accessible to and dependent on the automobile to "make it work." Imitations sprang up everywhere, gorging on the rich alluvial farmland that had earlier brought agricultural prosperity to the Toronto hinterland. Often, the nucleus of a community grew around shopping. The same year that saw the launching of Don Mills saw the opening of Sunnybrook, Ontario's first planned shopping centre at the corner of Eglinton and Bayview, strategically sited to benefit from the growth of the adjacent suburb of Leaside. The idea was revolutionary: you parked your car in a safe, paved and well-lit lot and then went about all your shopping needs in timely, convenient fashion. A year later the same private firm that put up Sunnyside created the Lawrence Plaza at Lawrence and Bathurst, and a year after that the Golden Mile at Eglinton and Victoria Park in what was then the Township of Scarborough. These beachheads were the forerunners of the hundreds of malls, from the humble roadside strips to the megasize monsters like Yorkdale, that characterize suburban Toronto today.

All of these developments — large and small, scattered over the city's environs in all directions — were private initiatives, but too often forgotten in the saga of their success is that they also relied fundamentally on public investment. The costs of creating infrastructure for these huge developments were colossal. Roads, arterial and internal, were just one part of a civic shopping list that included sewer and water pipes, hydro lines, gas mains, parks, schools and, of course, public transit, for although the suburbs might be the natural habitat of the automobile, not all of the inhabitants, particularly the very young and the old, had easy access to "a set of wheels." Moreover, the challenges of providing services to these new low-density, spread-out communities were astronomical compared with the densely concentrated mixed neighbourhoods of the old city. Who would pay for it all? Less concentration meant fewer taxpayers. Fewer taxpayers with higher taxes wasn't a popular projection for politicians. The bottom line could only be the creation of enormous public debt. This growing deficit might be — and was — ignored for a while in the fever of expansion, but some far-seeing officials and politicians felt that perhaps a new way of doing things would help.

CHANGING GOVERNMENT OR CHANGING GOVERNMENTS

Nothing characterizes Canadian public life so much as relentless intergovernmental tensions. From 1867, with the founding BNA Act, to today, we have been sorting out which level of government is responsible for what power. Is the upkeep of a certain road or other installation, for example, a federal, provincial, regional or municipal responsibility, or some complex combination of them all? Anyone looking at some of the laws and

Some say there are two seasons in Toronto — Winter and Construction. This view of cars driving along Lakeshore Boulevard East, looking west from Cherry Street, shows the Gardiner Expressway under construction.

regulations dating from the nineteenth century might wonder whether politicians ever conceived that the country might, sometime in the future, contain huge cities. Some founding fathers, like John A. Macdonald, considered that provinces should have no more powers than what he called glorified municipalities. The real question was — and remains — money and revenue, or, in short, who has the power to tax the poor benighted resident? The provinces eventually came out pretty well in their struggle with the federal government, but taxation powers for municipalities remain highly restricted and largely under the nanny-like tutelage of the provinces. So it was for Toronto — at least until very recently — with the bulk of revenues needed to cover the huge costs of expansion arising principally from property taxes.

If you couldn't raise more money, however, you might at least try to make government cheaper and more efficient through economies of scale and centralization of authority. Such was the thinking behind the creation of Metro Toronto in 1953.

It seems singularly Canadian to solve a governmental problem by creating yet another level of government, but in many ways the Municipality of Metropolitan Toronto worked well. It came about, again in good Canadian fashion, from the work of a Royal Commission, which recommended two-tier government as the solution for the mushrooming city. Like the Canadian federation itself, the new, larger civic government would look after regional issues, while the old constituent local governments tended to traditionally local affairs. What were these communities? At the heart was the City of Toronto itself, then the outlying semi-rural places like North York, Scarborough, York and Etobicoke, then some of the smaller semi-urban communities like Long Branch, Mimico, New Toronto, Swansea, Weston, and finally the better-established East York, Leaside and wealthy Forest Hill. By the mid-1960s the province further welded the smaller bits of this amalgam into one City of Toronto plus the five *boroughs* of North York, Etobicoke, York, East York and Scarborough, each of which, except East York, eventually abandoned that label and called themselves cities with a capital C.

Metro Toronto was a success, although a qualified one. There were great advantages to consolidating police and fire departments or to creating a vast regional system of parks. Monies were saved and efficiency increased. But there were critics too. Inevitably, another level of government required another level of pricey bureaucracy. And to the consternation of many, the all-powerful Chair of the Metro Council was not elected by the citizenry of Metro at large, but elevated to the post by the backslapping votes of regional representatives. Was that democracy? And there was endless squabbling over jurisdictional powers, the most vigorous battle being over what to do with the Toronto Islands. Metro wanted them to be converted solely to park use, but the City of Toronto, within whose boundaries they were located, urged some retention for traditional (and coveted) residential sites. Compromises satisfied no one.

But, generally speaking, the provincial government smiled on its creation of Metropolitan Toronto. Within a few years it instituted more regional governments throughout the province, like Hamilton–Wentworth and Ottawa–Carleton. Cities remained, however, the creatures of the province — with the province acting not only as the ultimate banker, but also as the legal arbiter. Metro citizens chafed — and Torontonians still do — at the faceless Ontario Municipal Board that so often determined their local affairs.

Established first in 1906 as the Ontario Railway and Municipal Board, this independent provincial administrative tribunal eventually dropped the railway function and now hears appeals relating to land-use planning, development, land expropriation and municipal finance. It also has arbitrational powers with regard to about seventy additional public statutes.

Whatever its strengths and weaknesses Metro seemed a permanent part of Toronto's identity. Its brand was everywhere — the Metro Central Library, the Metro Archives, the Metro Police — and newspapers and other media frequently took to labelling the locals by the title "Metro woman" or "Metro man." It wasn't destined to go on forever, but it would last almost half a century.

WATERSHEDS

It is challenging to conceive of a single date or event that marks what might be called the emergence of *modern* or *contemporary* Toronto. Social change is always gradual, almost imperceptible to those caught up in the stream. But certain events and achievements are symbolic, and for Toronto the pace of events quickened in the 1960s. The basis was there: diverse migration and immigration, solid prosperity and a flourishing Canadian economy, with Toronto as its capstone, and more efficient and seemingly progressive government. There were also other nascent achievements that would prove both far-reaching and very influential on the city: television production began in 1952 and Toronto's output soon led the country; the subway came in 1954 and revolutionized access, especially in winter months; Highway 401, then called the Toronto Bypass, soon proved a vital internal link as much as a road to somewhere else; and the mighty baby boom massively came of age, or at least of an age where its numerical strength and economic power were increasingly felt — anybody listening to CHUM

Toronto had toyed with the idea of a subway as early as 1909 but decades passed before the dream became a reality and it wasn't until 1949 that construction finally began on what many called "the Yonge Street Ditch." This 1952 painting by Eric Freifeld shows work just north of College. The line, 4.6 miles long, opened to the public on March 30, 1954.

radio's rock and roll touched that pulse.

The 1960s brought it all together. By then the population of the Toronto region was more than two and a half million.

Architecture was iconic in terms of a new way of doing things, and the most definitive structure for the new Toronto was Viljo Revell's new City Hall of 1965. The Finnish architect was the hands-down winner of an international competition, but it was not just the graceful, curved double towers that won both critical and popular acclaim — it was the bounded civic square that graced the design and, for the first time ever, gave a civic heart to Toronto. Here was an open place where people might gather for events great and small, where the city might greet those from away and celebrate its own. In the words of the cultural critic Robert Fulford, Toronto had a living room.

So at last symbolism matched reality. And soon other architectural monuments augmented Revell's modernism: Mies Van der Rohe's Toronto–Dominion Centre, Ron Thom's Massey College, the showpiece Ontario Place, and then a slew of formidable bank buildings, with the whole effort not long after capped by the CN Tower and rooted by SkyDome, now the Rogers Centre, at its foot. Already the arts were served by the commodious O'Keefe Centre, the renovated gem of the Royal Alexandra Theatre, and Hart House theatre at the University of Toronto. These cultural landmarks would soon be joined by a reinvigorated Art Gallery of Toronto (relabelled and refinanced as the Art Gallery of Ontario), the Ontario Science Centre in Don Mills, the Metro Toronto Zoo, Roy Thomson Hall, and the St. Lawrence Centre for the Performing Arts. Previously, few Torontonians would have considered that the arts paid off financially — but they did, and not just for themselves but through augmented tourism and huge growth in hotels, restaurants and bars. On this base, within a few years an "Entertainment District" grew up in the central city, dotted with a huge array of clubs, pubs and bistros reflecting the ethnic mix of the Toronto cosmopolis. By the end of the century the skyline of the central city would be almost unrecognizable to the denizens of 1945 — except perhaps for the bulk of the Royal York hotel opposite the town gate of Union Station. And still to come were the signature structures that make up the contemporary city: the Ontario College of Art and Design — a matchbox on stilts to some but still an engineering marvel, Frank Gehry's redesign of the Art Gallery, at long last a sleek and spacious air terminal, the expanded Gardiner Ceramics Museum, the new crystalline face given to the Royal Ontario Museum, and not least the Four Seasons Centre for the Performing Arts, the long-coveted Opera House, where the structure at last matched the quality of the performers.

There are other ways to measure achievement amongst Toronto's multicultural millions, from the success of professional sports (baseball and basketball being added to the traditional football and hockey, with a renewed interest in international soccer) to a growth in higher education (three universities, a new and welcoming central reference library and dozens of research centres), to enthusiastic annual celebrations of unity in diversity (Caribana, Caravan and Gay Pride).

But it didn't just happen. A vigorous economy served as the platform for all the success and growth. Toronto became a financial centre, with the old industries that had provided earlier prosperity retreating to distant suburbs and other communities — indeed, to other countries. It was more than just population growth that allowed Toronto to snatch the crown of Canada's largest city away from Montreal. Toronto by the 1960s was the unchallenged money capital. The growth of financial services, the relocation of head offices of banks and insurance companies to the city, the extension of the Toronto Stock Exchange beyond

Above: The old Registry Office, with its massive Corinthian columns, was erected in 1917 and was to be a part of a large civic centre plan that simply never happened. Here, poignantly juxtaposed with the new City Hall, it is being torn down while the new building goes up. Efforts to move the massive old structure had proved fruitless.
Right: City Hall today.

a mere list of mining ventures, the concentration of intellectual power and all the attendant needs of these initiatives built a huge service economy, one that gobbled up brawn and brain. But there were also some welcome shackles on this unparalleled development. Again, certain events are emblematic: the coming of voluble and influential

The first Blue Jays game was not washed out by rain but might have been stopped by a white-out. The date: April 7, 1977. The place: Exhibition Stadium. The white stuff in the background: snow, as well-remembered by the opening day crowd of near 45,000.

Right: The Rogers Centre, home of the Blue Jays, viewed from the CN Tower.

urban critic Jane Jacobs to the city in 1968; the truncation of the Spadina Expressway; the protection of key neighbourhoods like the Beach, the Islands or the Annex; and the election of responsive city councils able to compromise with business leaders instead of engaging in prolonged trench warfare.

ALL POLITICS ARE LOCAL?

Progressivism in city politics? There's a theme of long standing. The Urban Reform movements of the early twentieth century sought to put the running of the city in the hands of apolitical efficiency experts. As a result, a large and competent urban civil service grew up, one that was greatly extended with the emergence of Metro government, starting in 1953. Municipal responsibilities had multiplied. The Metro system more and more resembled Canadian federalism, with concerns such as education, welfare, transport, and police and fire coming under the aegis of the government while the old city and the other constituent parts of Metro looked after more local tasks. As with Canadian federalism, there was plenty of opportunity for rancour and uncertainty over jurisdiction. Resentments grew along with the growth of outlying districts, especially as their collective powers — and their right to elect the Metro chairman — gave them more and more clout. Many in the old city rankled at the arrangement.

Toronto, in the 1960s and 1970s, wasn't alone

The trading floor of the Toronto Stock Exchange painted in 1973 by William Kurelek. Toronto has had a recognized stock exchange since 1878 and for many of the tumultuous years of the twentieth century the action was in this room in an Art Deco building erected in 1937 on Bay Street.

in questioning the idea that bigger was always going to be better. "People power" was a theme of the time; there was open questioning of the rights of big government or big bureaucracy to direct the everyday affairs of citizens. Unrestricted growth was openly debated, the rule of the automobile opposed, the preservation of old neighbourhoods championed. In the Toronto core the enthusiasm was boosted by a couple of scrappy mayors — David Crombie and John Sewell — plus motivated city councils. Crombie, dubbed the "Tiny Perfect Mayor," presided from 1973 to 1978, and the more aggressive Sewell, known as "Mayor Blue Jeans," held the reins from 1978 to 1980. Under Crombie, Toronto imposed a forty-foot limit on new buildings, celebrated neighbourhoods and successfully harnessed unchecked development. Sewell, from the vantage point of his bicycle seat, took this humanization of the city further, but his strong leftist ideological stances openly alienated big business, commerce and industry, much of which fled to the more tolerant and lower-taxed suburbs. The new urban reformers were eventually displaced in subsequent elections by more conservative politicians, but they had accomplished at least one significant thing — they had assured that urban planning would be more than an academic study, that citizens, especially in the old city, had to be consulted if a government were to be successful.

Toronto politics, in fact most Canadian urban politics, was characterized by the non-involvement of the country's major political parties. That didn't mean that city politicians were uncommitted — simply that the banner was not officially waved. But the influences were there: the inner city most frequently voted leftist NDP and the outlying jurisdictions supported Liberals or Conservatives.

That split between inner and outer became most evident with the election of Michael Harris's Tory provincial government in 1995. These were not the compromising brokerage Ontario Tories of old. The aim of the so-called "Common Sense Revolution" was classic neo-conservatism: smaller government, fewer and lower taxes and a balanced budget. And how to do it? Cut services, trim the civil service, shut down hospitals, transfer social-welfare costs to municipal jurisdictions and consolidate — most significantly, consolidate Metro Toronto by scrapping the Metro concept and creating one "megacity." And so it was done, for the province had the power, and with the old City kicking and screaming, it went into effect at the beginning of 1998. Community Councils now represent the vintage constituent parts of Metro and elect members who, with the mayor, make up an Executive Council. Old Toronto remains the largest Community Council with, at least theoretically, the most power, but the 'burbs are collectively more influential than ever.

A central problem remains for Toronto, and it is one that confronts most Ontario urban areas. The city is continually in deficit. The property tax base is not sufficient to finance the multiplex needs of a modern metropolis. The plurality of power is retained by the province, and although occasionally that senior government may bail out the city or permit a minor expansion of its tax base, the provincial government does not see cities as the engines that drive the province — socially, politically and economically. And, of course, Toronto drives most of all. A solution to the fiscal problem is critical.

SEEN AND HEARD
Of Toronto in the 1980s, the Montreal cartoonist Terry Mosher, better known as Aislin,

Right: The Dream of Mayor Crombie in Glenstewart Ravine, *painted by William Kurelek in 1974.*

Artist Carlos Marchiori, in his painting Bloor Street West, *captures perfectly the vibrant cityscape looking west at Bloor and Yonge in 1976.*

The Four Seasons Centre for the Performing Arts — home to the Canadian Opera Company and the National Ballet of Canada — opened in 2006.

observed: "It's the only city I know where people leap out of bed and yell, 'Thank God it's Monday!'" The actor Peter Ustinov famously called the place "a kind of New York operated by the Swiss." American newspaper columnist George Will called it "a modern miracle — a city that has become better as it has become bigger." Torontonians took pleasure in these remarks. They saw no tension between themselves as people who enjoyed living and working in a city that itself "worked." Toronto was the centre of the country — in terms of the economy, of at least English-speaking society and of, in a broad definition, English Canadian culture. Toronto had the National Ballet, the Canadian Opera Company, the largest university, the most extensive concentration of galleries, four daily newspapers, four national TV networks and a plurality of publishing houses. Immigrants continued to flock to the place, attracted by jobs and in many cases an already resident family. But their origins had changed: from European to Asian and South Asian with a strong sprinkling of Latin American. The city, as a result, boasted shamelessly that it was the most multicultural on

the planet and tried to overlook the unpleasant fact that some of Toronto's ethnic communities brought their problems and tensions with them.

Since Toronto's society comprised elements from all over the world, local boosters during the 1990s began calling the place a "world city." Flattering, at least to some, but not true. Toronto was not the equivalent of old Imperial centres like London, Paris or Tokyo, nor did it wield the socio-economic power of new world cities like New York. It was not the seat of an ancient civilization, such as Delhi, or a place where despotic power had reigned over millions, like Moscow, or a place desperately trying to reinvent itself, like Beijing. What it was was something more attractive to most of the world's inhabitants: safe, prosperous, predictable, substantial, decent. In short, it was a good place to live in a country that could boast the same qualities.

While not being a global power broker, Toronto could, however, claim many of the attributes of world cities. Like them, it had morphed into a private and public administrative centre where people toiled, in one way or another, in a gigantic service economy. What had remained of

Ontario Place, a seasonal entertainment and amusement park conceived to help revitalize the Toronto waterfront, opened in 1971. One of its many events is the spectacular Chinese Lantern Festival, held August through October.

manufacturing had largely fled to the outermost suburbs and the fields beyond — except for the products of what the nineteenth century had called "brain workers" — the high-tech industries (although many of them were arguably part of the service industry as well). Cultural standards had gone way beyond the occasional celebrated pianist filling the Eaton Auditorium. Toronto, if not a world centre, could claim world class music, opera, dance and theatre. Its educational system had produced Nobel laureates, globally applauded writers, acclaimed academics and innovative business leaders. By the turn of the twenty-first century, the near two and a half million people who called themselves Torontonians (and even the five million who lived in the GTA, the Greater Toronto Area) could revel in the plaudits awarded by outsiders, the *Economist* magazine repeatedly declaring the city one of the most desirable places to live in the world.

THE PERSONIFICATION OF TORONTO

Cities have been personified from the ancient Greeks through Charles Dickens's celebrated tale of Paris and London to contemporary times. What to call today's Toronto? Cinderella comes to mind. Certainly she seems lower-born than her more glamorous North American siblings like New York, Montreal or San Francisco (which actually did ascend from the cinders). She works hard, stays in the background, is often overlooked, but underneath is full of strength and beauty. But Toronto has yet to be invited to the ball (meaning hosting the Olympics or a World's Fair) let alone to wear the glass slipper and marry the prince. And who would be the Fairy godmother — definitely not the provincial government?

Toronto is certainly not risqué, a *femme fatale*, like her Gallic sister, Montreal. Or pushy, like masculine New York. Or sham, like Las Vegas.

Critics and the populace at large remain divided over the success of the Michael Lee-Chin Crystal — the pointy exuberance by Polish-born American architect Daniel Libeskind which bursts out between two staid wings of the old Royal Ontario Museum. Good, grey Toronto is nowhere in sight in this lively photo of the opening night.

Toronto's real personification may be that of a middle-aged, middle-class aunt or uncle, ungendered but recognizably human, and wearing sensible shoes: wise, experienced, still capable of turning heads, but both world-wary and a little world-weary.

But tempting as it is to compare a city to a person — most city histories almost invariably read like biographies — it is too much of a simplification. And personification can lead to a kind of self-satisfaction, which is exactly what contemporary Toronto does not need. The urban challenges that face Toronto are not unique. What could make Toronto different from other cities might be the way the city tackles these global issues.

It was the land that attracted people to settle here in the first place. If you climb to the top of the CN Tower and look north, west and east you see increasing sprawl over what were once the best farmlands in Canada. The GTA population of five million plus likely will be almost three million more in the next quarter-century. That growth will gobble up what remains of the farms and increase our dependence on the automobile. What is called "smart growth" would redevelop what has already been developed: rework the old strip malls, renovate the abandoned industrial lands, activate the myriad lanes that parallel our major streets to provide mixed housing, and do it all within a public transportation grid. The condo tower is not the answer, any more than the high-rise rental was for an earlier generation. Condo-style ownership of low-rise buildings is another matter, and brings a more human dimension to the city. At the same time, we have to ask why and how people come here — visitors and residents alike. Cities were originally surrounded by walls, with gates to control traffic and enhance defence. Later, when cities welcomed people, when, as the medieval phrase had it, town air made men free, the gates were made welcoming and symbolized the promises of freedom and potential prosperity that were within.

Rowan Gillespie's stark and striking sculptures form part of the contemporary memorial for the Irish Famine victims, many of whom made their way to Canada in the mid-nineteenth century, a reminder that Toronto remains a refuge for those from abroad.

Old Union Station has that symbolic function still, ushering people into the inner city, but Toronto's hyper-efficient, soulless modern major air terminal could be anywhere, and doesn't even have a sign to point visitors downtown. Smarter growth also means taking advantage of what you already have. Few cities in the world have the rich, cultural distinctions of Toronto in one package — but for the casual visitor this city of neighbourhoods remains mostly the downtown core, a downtown that acts too frequently as the anonymous stand-in for any number of American cities in films. The city needs to reinvent itself so that it is not merely a legal entity called Toronto, but a significant, distinctive place, where there is a unity in the diversity of its peoples and neighbourhoods.

There are some signs that this need for reinvention — and there must be continual reinvention — is being recognized. One of the lamentations frequently heard is that, although Toronto is a vital financial centre, it lacks the aggressive venture capitalists of the American model. Torontonians are rightly reticent about carelessly pursuing risk, but a bolder approach to marrying thoughtful planning to assertive investment might provide a tonic. Recently, a partnership between the city, the province, the federal government and private enterprise gave Toronto a spanking new soccer stadium — for the use of amateurs and professionals alike. It couldn't have been done without *all* of the partners. The same kind of partnerships are being talked about for the renewal of Nathan Phillips Square. Private and public money are also being used in commercial projects, like the massive new sound stage being designed on disused waterfront lands by Will Alsop, the architect who has already given us the distinctive Ontario College of Art and Design. Compromise need not lead to complacency.

At the outset of this book, Peter Carruthers argued that Toronto has always represented a kind of physical and cultural *middle ground* — from the time of the Native and fur traders' Toronto Passage north to Lake Simcoe, through the mixture of French and British soldiers and settlers, to the multicultural mélange that characterizes the place today. The middle ground in human affairs is where balanced discussion occurs and where successful, productive solutions are found. Clearly, as this collection of essays shows, Toronto has always, and generally successfully, sought that middle ground. The result is a vibrant present, but it is up to the present to assure the opportunity for a worthwhile future.

FURTHER READING

Aitken, Gail, and Donald F. Bellamy. *A History of the Children's Aid Society of Toronto*. Toronto: Dundurn Press, 2000.

Allen, Max, ed. *Ideas That Matter: The Worlds of Jane Jacobs*. Owen Sound: The Ginger Press, 1997.

Anthony, Ian. *Radio Wizard: Edward Samuel Rogers and the Revolution in Communications*. Toronto: Gage and Rogers Communications, 2000.

Armstrong, Frederick Henry. *A City in the Making: People and Perils in Victorian Toronto*. Toronto: Dundurn Press, 1988.

Arthur, Eric. *Toronto: No Mean City*. Third edition, revised by Stephen A. Otto. Toronto: University of Toronto Press, 1986.

Ashdown, Dana William. *Iron and Steam: A History of the Locomotive and Railway Car Builders of Toronto*. Toronto: Robin Brass Studio, 1999.

Barsky, Lesley Marrus. *From Generation to Generation: A History of Toronto's Mount Sinai Hospital*. Toronto: McClelland and Stewart, 1998.

Benn, Carl. *Historic Fort York, 1793–1993*. Toronto: Natural Heritage Books, 1993.

Berchem, F.R. *The Yonge Street Story, 1793–1860: An Account from Letters, Diaries and Newspapers*. Toronto: Natural Heritage Books, 1996.

_____. *Opportunity Road: Yonge Street, 1860–1939*. Toronto: Natural Heritage Books, 1996.

Breton, Raymond, et al. *Ethnic Identity and Equality: Varieties of Experience in a Canadian City*. Toronto: University of Toronto Press, 1990.

Burr, Christina. *Spreading the Light: Work and Labour Reform in Late-Nineteenth-Century Toronto*. Toronto: University of Toronto Press, 1999.

Careless, J.M.S. *Toronto to 1918*. First published 1984. Toronto: James Lorimer, 2002.

City of Toronto. *A Glimpse of Toronto's History: Opportunities for the Commemoration of Lost Historic Sites*. Toronto: City of Toronto and the Toronto Historical Association, 2001.

Cochrane, Jean. *Kensington*. Erin: Boston Mills Press, 2000.

Connor, J.T.H. *Doing Good: The Life of Toronto's General Hospital in the 19th and 20th Centuries*. Toronto: University of Toronto Press, 2000.

Coopersmith, Penina. *Cabbagetown: The Story of a Victorian Neighbourhood*. Toronto: James Lorimer, 1998.

Crawford, Bess Hillary. *Rosedale*. Erin: Boston Mills Press, 2000.

Dale, Clare A. *The Palaces of Government: A History of the Legislative Buildings of the Provinces of Upper Canada, Canada, and Ontario, 1792–1992*. Toronto: Ontario Legislative Library, 1993.

Darke, Eleanor. *A Mill Should Be Build Thereon: An Early History of Todmorden Mills*. Toronto: Natural Heritage Books, 1995.

Dendy, William. *Lost Toronto*. Revised edition. Toronto: McClelland and Stewart, 1992.

Dieterman, Frank A., and Ronald F. Williamson. *Government on Fire: the History and Archaeology of Upper Canada's First Parliament Buildings*. Toronto: eastendbooks, 2001.

Ellis, Chris J., and Neal Ferris, eds. *The Archaeology of Southern Ontario to A.D. 1650*. London: London Chapter, Archaeological Society of Ontario, 1990.

Fagan, Cary, and Robert MacDonald, eds. *Streets of Attitude: Toronto Stories*. Toronto: ECW Press, 1990.

Filey, Mike. *Not a One-Horse Town: 125 Years of Toronto and Its Streetcars*. Willowdale: Firefly Books, 1990.

_____. *Toronto Sketches: The Way We Were* [and subsequent volumes]. Toronto: Dundurn Press, 1992.

_____. *From Horse Power to Horsepower: Toronto, 1880–1930*. Toronto: Dundurn Press, 1993.

_____, et al. *Toronto, Then and Now*. Ottawa: Magic Light, 2000.

Firth, Edith G., ed. *The Town of York, 1793–1815: A Collection of Documents of Early Toronto*. Toronto: Champlain Society, for the Government of Ontario, 1962.

_____. *The Town of York, 1815–1834: A Further Collection of Documents of Early Toronto*. Toronto: Champlain Society, for the Government of Ontario, 1966.

Frager, Ruth. *Sweatshop Strife: Class, Ethnicity, and Gender in the Jewish Labour Movement of Toronto, 1900–1939*. Toronto: University of Toronto Press, 1992.

Friedland, Martin. *The University of Toronto: A History*. Toronto: University of Toronto Press, 2002.

Fulford, Robert. *Accidental City: The Transformation of Toronto*. Toronto: MacFarlane, Walter, and Ross, 1995.

_____. *Toronto Discovered*. Toronto: Key Porter Books, 1998.

Gatenby, Greg. *Toronto: A Literary Guide*. Toronto: McArthur and Company, 1999.

Giles, Wenona. *Portuguese Women in Toronto: Gender, Immigration, and Nationalism*. Toronto: University of Toronto Press, 2002.

Harris, Richard. *Unplanned Suburbs: Toronto's American Tragedy, 1900 to 1950*. Baltimore: Johns Hopkins University Press, 1996.

Hart, Patricia. *Pioneering in North York: A History of the Borough*. Toronto: General Publishing, 1968.

Iacovetta, Franca. *Such Hardworking People: Italian Immigrants in Postwar Toronto*. Montreal and Kingston: McGill–Queen's University Press, 1992.

Johnson, Leo A. "The Mississauga–Lake Ontario Land Surrender of 1805." *Ontario History* 83/3 (1990).

Johnston, Denis W. *Up the Mainstream: The Rise of Toronto's Alternative Theatres, 1968–1975*. Toronto: University of Toronto Press, 1991.

Jones, Donald. *Fifty Tales of Toronto*. Toronto: University of Toronto Press, 1992.

Kapches, Mima. "Beyond Archaeology on the Ancient Beaten Paths of Toronto." Royal Ontario Museum *Archaeological Newsletter*, Series 2/40 (1990).

Kilbourn, William. *Intimate Grandeur: 100 Years at Massey Hall*. Don Mills: Stoddart, 1993.

Killan, Gerald. *David Boyle: From Artisan to Archaeologist*. Toronto: University of Toronto Press, 1983.

Lemon, James. *Toronto Since 1918*. First published 1985. Toronto: James Lorimer, 2002.

Leonetti, Mike. *Maple Leaf Legends: 75 Years of Toronto's Hockey Heroes*. Vancouver: Raincoast Books, 2002.

Lundell, Liz. *The Estates of Old Toronto*. Erin: Boston Mills Press, 1997.

MacDonald, Jeanne, et al. *Toronto Women: Changing Faces, 1900–2000: A Photographic Journey*. Toronto: eastendbooks, 1997.

MacDougall, Heather. *Activists and Advocates: Toronto's Health Department, 1883–1993*. Toronto: Dundurn Press, 1990.

MacIntosh, Robert, M. *Earliest Toronto*. Refrew: General Store Publishing House, 2006.

Malcomson, Robert. *Capital in Flames: the American Attack on York, 1813*. Montreal: Robin Brass Studio, 2008.

Mays, John Bentley. *Emerald City: Toronto Visited*. Toronto: Penguin Books, 1994.

McGowan, Mark G. *The Waning of the Green: Catholics, the Irish, and Identity in Toronto, 1887–1922*. Montreal and Kingston: McGill–Queen's University Press, 1999.

_____. *Michael Power: The Struggle to Build the Catholic Church on the Canadian Frontier*. Montreal: McGill-Queen's University Press, 2007.

McLuhan, Elizabeth, ed. *Safe Haven: The Refugee Experience of Five Families*. Toronto: Multicultural Historical Society of Ontario, 1995.

McQueen, Rod. *The Eatons: The Rise and Fall of Canada's Royal Family*. Revised edition. Toronto: Stoddart, 1999.

Miller, Ian. *Our Glory and Our Grief: Torontonians and the Great War*. Toronto: University of Toronto Press, 2002.

Robertson, John Ross. *Landmarks of Toronto: A Collection of Historical Sketches of the Old Town of York from 1792 to 1833 and of Toronto from 1834*. 6 vols. Toronto: the author, 1894–1914.

Robinson, Percy J. *Toronto During the French Régime*. First published 1933. Toronto: University of Toronto Press, 1965.

Russell, Victor, ed. *Forging a Consensus: Historical Essays on Toronto*. Toronto: Toronto Sesquicentennial Board and the University of Toronto Press, 1984.

Scadding, Henry. *Toronto of Old: Collections and Recollections, Illustrative of the Early Settlement and Social Life of the Capital of Ontario*. Toronto: Adam, Stephenson, 1873.

Schabas, Ezra, and Carl Moray. *Opera Viva: The Canadian Opera Company: The First 50 Years*. Toronto: Dundurn Press, 2000.

Sewell, John. *Doors Open Toronto: Illuminating the City's Great Spaces*. Toronto: Knopf, 2002.

Seymour, Murray. *Toronto's Ravines: Walking the Hidden Country*. Erin: Boston Mills Press, 2000.

Shadd, Adrienne, Afua Cooper, and Karolyn Smardz Frost. *The Underground Railway: Next Stop, Toronto!* Toronto: Natural Heritage Books, 2002.

Shapiro, Linda. *Yesterday's Toronto, 1870–1910.* Revised edition. North Vancouver: Waterlane Editions, 1997.

Smardz Frost, Karolyn, *I've Got a Home in Glory Land: A Lost Tale of the Underground Railroad.* Toronto: Thomas Allen, 2007.

Steckley, John, "Toronto . . . or is that Taranteau?" in *Explore Historic Toronto*, Toronto Historical Board, November 1992.

Strange, Carolyn. *Toronto's Girl Problem: The Perils and Pleasures of the City, 1880–1930.* Toronto: University of Toronto Press, 1995.

Tanner, Helen Hornbeck, ed. *Atlas of Great Lakes Indian History.* Norman: University of Oklahoma Press, 1987.

Thomas, Jocko. *From Police Headquarters: True Tales from the Big City Crime Beat.* Toronto: Stoddart, 1990.

Toper, Harold. *History of Immigration Since the Second World War: From Toronto "The Good" to Toronto "The World in a City."* Toronto: Joint Centre of Excellence for Research on Immigration, 2000.

Toronto Illustrated, 1893. First published 1893. Toronto: Ontario Genealogical Society, 1992.

Toronto Port Authority. *Toronto Harbour:, The Passing Years.* Toronto: TPA, 2002.

Trigger, Bruce G. *The Children of Aataentsic: A History of the Huron People to 1660.* Montreal and Kingston: McGill–Queen's University Press, 1976.

White, Randall. *Ontario Since 1985.* Toronto: eastendbooks, 1998.

_____. *Too Good to Be True: Toronto in the 1920s.* Toronto: Dundurn Press, 1993.

Wickson, Ted. *Reflections of Toronto Harbour: 200 Years of Port Activity and Waterfront Development.* Toronto: Toronto Port Authority, 2002.

Williamson, Ronald F., and David A. Robertson, eds. "The Archaeology of the Parsons Site: A Fifty Year Perspective." *Ontario Archaeology* 65/66 (1998).

Williamson, Ronald F., and Susan A. Pfeiffer, eds. "Bones of the Ancestors: The Archaeology and Osteobiography of the Moatfield Ossuary." Archaeological Survey of Canada, Canadian Museum of Civilization *Mercury Series Paper* 163 (2003).

CONTRIBUTORS

Christopher Andreae, PhD,
University of Western Ontario
President, Historica Research Ltd.

Dr. Andreae is a geographer and historian with dozens of years' experience in historical planning and research, especially in the areas of built heritage assessments and industrial archaeology. He has particular expertise in the fields of industrial and transportation history. Some of the projects he has undertaken in Toronto include heritage assessments of the railway lands south of Union Station, the Don Valley Brick Works, Gooderham & Worts Distillery and the Canada Malting complex. He is the author of the award-winning *Lines of Country: An Atlas of Railway and Waterway History in Canada* (1997).

Carl Benn, MDiv and PhD,
York University
Chair, History, Ryerson University

Dr. Benn is the Chair of the Department of History at Ryerson University, a position he took up recently after working in the museum field for thirty-four years, most recently as Chief Curator of the City of Toronto Museums and Heritage Services. He also taught undergraduate history and graduate museum studies at the University of Toronto for seventeen years. He is the author of *Historic Fort York, 1793-1993*; *The Iroquois in the War of 1812*; and *the War of 1812* along with dozens of other publications. Currently he is writing two books, one focused on Native memoirs from 1812-1815, and another on the Mohawks who participated in the Gordon Relief Expedition on the Nile River during the Sudan War of 1884-1885.

Peter J. Carruthers, MA,
University of Calgary
Senior Associate, Archaeological Services Inc.

Peter Carruthers served in the Ministry of Culture for twenty-seven years as a Heritage Planner and Environmental Assessment Coordinator before joining Archaeological Services Inc. as a Senior Associate in the Environmental Assessment Division. In government he was responsible for developing and administering programs related to heritage conservation, and he has undertaken extensive research and writing related to the development of the Province's regulatory system for the conservation of heritage sites and landscapes. He served as the Chair of Heritage Toronto from 2002 to 2007.

Roger Hall, PhD,
Cambridge University
Chair, History, University of Western Ontario

Dr. Hall is Graduate Chair in History at the University of Western Ontario, where he has been a faculty member for more than three decades. He has published widely in Canadian, and especially Ontario, history in both scholarly and popular media. He has been Editor of *Ontario History*, the journal of the Ontario Historical Society, and Co-editor of *The Canadian Review of American Studies*, and he is currently General Editor of the Champlain Society. As well, he has been a Visiting Fellow at Clare Hall, Cambridge University, and is now a Senior Fellow at Massey College, University of Toronto.

Robert I. MacDonald, PhD,
McGill University
Partner and Senior Archaeologist,
Archaeological Services Inc.

Dr. MacDonald has over twenty-five years of field and administrative experience with the archaeology of the Great Lakes region. He has served as the Deputy Director of the Quaternary Sciences Institute at the University of Waterloo and is an Adjunct Assistant Professor in the Department of Anthropology at the University of Waterloo as well as a Research Associate of the Trent University Archaeological Research Centre. His special areas of expertise include Iroquoian archaeology, ecological archaeology, archaeological site potential modelling, and geographic information system (GIS) applications in archaeology.

Ronald F. Williamson, PhD,
McGill University
Managing Partner and Chief Archaeologist,
Archaeological Services Inc.

Dr. Williamson is an archaeologist with over thirty-five years of field and research experience. In 1980, he founded Archaeological Services Inc., which has grown to become the largest archaeological consulting firm in Canada. He has administered and directed hundreds of archaeological assessments, excavations and heritage planning studies, and he is the Director of the multi-year Master Plan of Archaeological Resources for the City of Toronto. He is also an Associate of the Graduate Faculty at the University of Toronto and has published extensively on the pre-contact and post-contact history of northeastern North America. A former president of the Canadian Association of Professional Heritage Consultants, he served on the board of Heritage Toronto from 2001 to 2007.

ILLUSTRATION CREDITS

The authors would like to thank the many archivists, curators, institutions, librarians and individuals who supplied images for this book. All attempts to find copyright holders have been made and any errors brought to the publisher's attention will be corrected in future editions.
L=left R=right B=bottom T=top M=middle

48th Highlanders of Canada Museum: 101; 1680 Lac Ontario ou de Frontenac - Lac de Toronto: 51; Angel Art Photography: 56, 57; Archaeological Services Inc.: 13, 29, 36, 37R, 42, 46L, 46R, 48. Andrea Carnevale: 5, 31T, 31M, 45, 47TR, 47BL. Andrew Clish: 40L. Sarina Finlay: 24L. John Howarth: 52. Shelley Huson: 25, 35T. Robert Pihl: 30. David Robertson: 49. Andrea Williams: 43, 119. Ronald F. Williamson: 37L; Archaeological Services Inc., Ska nah Doht, Longwoods Road Conservation Area: 38. Ronald F. Willamson: 39, 44T, 44B; Archives of Ontario: 62 (map by David W. Smith, C2790-0-0-34), 66 (F47-11-1-0-107), 77 (Series 15333), 85 (I0016056), 98 (I0005419); Art Gallery of Ontario: 67 (52/32); Yarema Bezchlibnyk, Private Collection: 120; Courtesy of Dave Birrell at the Nanton Lancaster Society Air Museum in Alberta, Canada: 100T; Canadian Opera Company's Four Seasons Centre for the Performing Arts in Toronto: 117 (Sam Javanrouh); Carnevale Family, Private Collection: 104L; Hsiang Cheng, Private Collection: 118; City of Toronto Archives (Fonds or Series followed by Item number): 7L (1244, 161), 7M (1244, 1537), 7R (648, Files 093, id003), 8 (1244, 1237), 72B (SC 655-1), 80 (1231, 677), 86L (1568, 356), 86R (1244, 002), 89 (0071, 2617), 90 (372, Sub-Series 32, 40), 99 (John H. Boyd, 1266, 96241), 100BL (1266, 102216), 103 (648, File 130, 004), 105 (497, 845010), 107 (1257, Series 1057, 5619), 111T (1268, 462); City of Toronto Art Collection, Culture, painting by John George Howard: 81; City of Toronto Museums and Heritage Services: 54 (Richard Gerrard), 71; Martin S. Cooper, Private Collection: 40R, 112L (Courtesy of the Toronto Blue Jays and Major League Baseball); Early Images: A Collection of Illustrations From Popular Sources Published Prior to 1923 http://www.copyrightexpired.com/earlyimage/index.html: 26; Rashid Farrah, Private Collection: 104B; Fort Ontario State Historical Site: 55T; William F. Fox, Private Collection: 34, 35B; Ed Freeman, Private Collection: 14; Tim Hagen, Photographer and Danielle Pignataro at the Ontario Greenbelt Website Friends of the Greenbelt Foundation www.ourgreenbelt.ca: 18, 22; Hamilton Public Library Special Collections: 75; iStock Photo: 78 (John Carvahlo), 10 (Avishay Lindenfeld), 15 (Peter Spiro), 27M (Paul Tessier), 112R (Dragan Trifunovic); Vlastimil Juricek: 111BR; William Kurelek (1927-1977) *The Dream of Mayor Crombie in Glen Stewart Ravine*, 1974, mixed media on masonite 80.0 x 69.2 cm. Collection: The Corporation of the City of Toronto, 1978 City of Toronto Art Collection, Culture. Copyright: the Estate of William Kurelek, courtesy of the Wynick/Tuck Gallery, Toronto: 115; William Kurelek, (1927-1977) *Light Trading on the Toronto Stock Exchange*, 1973 mixed media on masonite 91.4 x 109.2 cm. Original collection: Loewen, Ondaatje, McCutcheon & Company Limited, Toronto. Copyright: the Estate of William Kurelek, courtesy of the Wynick/Tuck Gallery, Toronto: 113; Father J. Lafitau, *Moeurs des Sauvages Amerioquains* (1724) Champlain Society: 41; Library and Archives Canada: 53 (engraving by Joseph Stadler after an image by George Heriot, C-012781), 55R, 61 (C-014905), 63 (C-040137), 65 (C-007434), 70 (C-011234); Alex MacDonald, Private Collection: 104R; McCord Museum: 87; Mary Hastings Meyer, *View of Toronto*, 1855 City of Toronto Art Collection, Culture: 19; Kathy Mills, Private Collection: 16, 17; Susanne Milligan, Private Collection: 104T; Laura Mousseau, Nature Conservancy of Canada: 20; Museum of Ontario Archaeology - Wilfrid Jury Collection: 27R; 33T, 33B (Robert Pearce); *Picturesque Canada*, 1882: 21; *The Power of the Press: The Story of Early Canadian Printers and Publishers* by Chris Raible, James Lorimer & Company Ltd., Publishers, 2007. Photographed by Rob Skeoch at MacKenzie House: 68L; Toronto Economic Development, City of Toronto Arts Services - The Market Gallery: 73 (CT/MG-A85-31), 93 (A81-36); Toronto Port Authority Archives: 92 (PC1/1/5927); Toronto Public Library: 58 (TRL-1874), 59 (oil painting by Jean Laurent Mosnier, TRL-1516), 60 (TRL-10333), 69 (TRL-30086), 74 (TPL-jrr1115), 76 (TRL-10931), 83 (TPL-jrr1059), 94 (TRL-2545), 95 (TRL-11767), 96 (TRL-10321), 116 (TRL-979-32-1); Toronto Reference Library, D.W. Smith Papers: 64L (B15-87), 64R (B15-90); Toronto Transit Commission: 109 (Eric Freifeld); Steve Urszenyi, Private Collection: 23 ; Ulrich Welling, Private Collection: 9, 11; University of Toronto, University College Archives, painting by Sir Edmund Head, 1858-9: 79; Wikipedia Commons: 68R (no copyright), 24R (Maury Markowitz), 72T (Simon Pulsifer); Ronald F. Williamson, Private Collection: 32.

INDEX